Your Personal Passport to Success

How to Get Where You Want to Be

Christian H. Godefroy

Table of contents

Your Personal Passport to Success

How to Get Where You Want to Be

Christian H. Godefroy

© Club Positif 2016

ISBN ebook 978-2-37318-018-3

ISBN 978-2-37318-019-0

CHRISTIAN GODEFROY (1948-2012) is a specialist in positive thinking and auto-suggestion. He has given training seminars to over 6,000 senior company personnel around the world on self-confidence, communication and relaxation. He was also a specialist in self-hypnosis, copywriting and self-publishing.

INTRODUCTION

Before using a new computer or a camera you are sure to read the user's guide carefully in order to avoid problems. You can then take pride in making proper use of your equipment, which will probably give you many years of excellent service.

We possess everything we need to be happy, efficient, prosperous human beings, to enjoy good health and make a success of out lives. Why is it, then, that our lives so often become filled with misery, complexes, problems, discouragement and depression? Why is it that we so rarely seem able to really live, to relax and be happy?

Well, even if we started out in life with an excellent 'machine' at out disposal, no one provided us with a user's guide. You don't learn anything about the art of living at school. And if we are unhappy, it is simply because we make ourselves unhappy. We use only a tenth of the capacity of out 'machine'. And yet every one of us possesses untold, unexploited treasures and unlimited resources.

But it's never too late to learn!

WEEK 1 -- YOU'RE WORTH A HUNDRED TIMES MORE THAN YOU THINK

This book will teach you how to make better use of your 'machine' and become successful in all areas of your life. It contains a lot more than advice or recommendations. This is a practical course which will stay with you for the rest of your days, and which, in a short time, will guide you to the summit of the art of living and success.

Its chapters are simple and concrete, and contain numerous practical applications in areas like re-educating yourself and mastering day-to-day living. You won't be exposed to a lot of theoretical information. Of course, the method does explain what things like adaptation, self-confidence, happiness, relaxation and so on consist of. But above all it shows you how to adapt, how to have more self-confidence, how to be happy, how to relax.

It will help you discover for yourself exactly why you are worth a hundred times more than you think you are, since you already possess the key to your own liberation...

Getting started

1. Find a place where you can be alone for a while, in your bedroom, or some quiet place removed from noise, with no radio, music or television.
2. Sit down, get comfortable, and start reading the method out loud (this is very important).
3. Underline anything that strikes you as being important.
4. Answer the lesson's questionnaire and do the suggested exercises.
5. Continue in this way, covering one lesson per week.

We are about to begin working together on a method for success through personal development. This practical method requires no homework, no study, nor does it include any written exams. However, throughout your reading you will need a pencil. If you don't have one handy, stop reading right now and go and get one!

Whenever you read something that strikes you as important, underline it. Don't be afraid to 'mess up' these pages: they are there to help you.

We should state that this method of success through personal development is very easy to understand, as you will soon see for yourself.

The only long word, the only phrase that may be difficult to understand, has just been used: personal development. Let's take a quick look at what it means.

You know what psychology is, don't you? You also know that we can talk about psychology as applied to child education, to sales, industry, the workplace, and so on.

Personal development is psychology applied to the way you live. In other words, it is the art of living your everyday life.

So you aren't going to be exposed to any psychological theories, but rather you are going to 'live' what psychology teaches us.

And that is precisely what personal development is all about: a collection of techniques for living better; the art of living is a collection of techniques for fulfilling yourself.

Now, what exactly does living better mean? It means being in better health, enjoying your work more, doing a better job of raising your children, being happier in a relationship, being more successful in your understandings, being more efficient, becoming a happier person - in short, feeling better about yourself.

Let's do a little calculating. How old are you? (Write it down)

How many hours have you been alive? Multiply your age by 365 days, and then multiply that total by 24 (hours per day)

If you're 38 years old, you've lived just over 332,896 hours. Today you're starting work on a method for success that will take you about 30 hours to complete. That isn't much, compared to the 332,896 hours you've already lived. It's actually a tiny fraction of your time, isn't it.

What I'm getting at by mentioning these figures is the following:

1. This method for success isn't going to change your life in some magical way, in just a few hours. But it is actually going to transform you, without any miracles!

2. For the method to do its work of transformation, you must be patient and do what is suggested right through to the end. That's the only condition you have to meet in order to become a new person in just 30 days.

An initiation

This method is a beginning, a first step, an 'initiation'

to a better life. You know what an initiation is, I'm sure. Used by groups like the Masons or Knights of Columbus, initiations are rituals where slightly mysterious things take place, things which are kept secret and understood only by other initiates.

In this method for success, a few unusual, even extraordinary things are going to happen, which you should keep to yourself until such time as I say you can go ahead and talk about them. But, for the moment, not a word to anyone!

Why this vow of silence? Well, I'm going to tell you why right now, and I'm sure you'll see that the recommendation makes good sense.

1.   Human society is full of people who don't know much, but who pretend they know everything. These people will laugh at you, because it's a lot easier to laugh at others who are trying to improve themselves, instead of trying to improve their own lives. (Do you know anyone who fits the description?)

2.   You'll inevitably run into people who have never accomplished much themselves. They will try to prevent you from succeeding as well. Under the guise of helping or protecting you, they will do all they can to discourage your initiatives in the area of personal development.

Now let's look at the ways this method will be profitable for you. As I already said, this method is not theoretical. My role is simply to show you the path I myself have been following for some time now, not to 'teach' you anything whatsoever. **You already know everything I'm going to tell you**. Therefore, the success of the method doesn't depend on how skilled I am, but rather on how open you are to what I have to say. It depends entirely on how much you put into what we'll discuss and think about together during the weeks that follow.

Before pointing out certain 'virtues' that might hinder your progress, I'd like you to remember that in this method:

1. you're not going to learn anything new.
2. you're not going to learn anything new.
3. you're not going to learn anything new.
4. you're hot going to learn anything new...

Do you think that's funny? Well, it's true: you're not going to learn anything new.

What we are going to do is think together, and improve our lives based on our reflections.

For example, you know as well as I do that your physical state influences how you feel. I don't have to teach you that. You also know that a sick person who has a positive frame of mind is more likely to get better than someone who is both ill and discouraged. I don't have to teach you that, either. And you also know, as I do, that it is possible to live better. I don't have to teach you that.

Live better

The important question is, what do we have to do to live better? And that's why a method on the art of living and success can be very useful. Because it teaches us how. That's what's new to us, and that is what we really need to learn:

- How to feel good;
- How to adapt better;
- How to have more self-confidence;
- How to relax;
- How to be more enthusiastic;
- How to be a happier person;
- And so on...

Now let's have a little fun and look at some of the 'viruses' that may hinder our efforts on the path to success. Don't think that this is a waste of time. On the contrary, always remember that before you plant your seeds you have to prepare the soil.

Some of these viruses may continue threatening your progress throughout the course of the method. Su if something you read in the method bothers you, ask yourself if you exhibit any symptoms of the following viruses (I'm going to describe just a few - you may very well discover some of your own!).

Intellectual myelitis

Symptoms: an insatiable need to acquire information and intellectualize everything in sight. Less serious if subjects have an average education, but chronic if they happen to be carrying around a certain amount of intellectual baggage, bloated with university degrees. Once again I repeat: we aren't going to learn anything new here. So if, after your first week, you find yourself saying, 'But I knew all that already!' don't forget to add:

> **'What I already knew I am now going to put into practice in my everyday lire.'**

'Throwing in the towel' syndrome

This virus causes sufferers to give up before finishing anything. Remember: the method can produce extraordinary results, but to obtain them you have to stick with it faithfully right to the end. Tell yourself: I've been waiting for an opportunity like this for too long, I'll stick with it no matter what.'

> **'I'll stick with it no matter what happens.'**

Chronic doubt syndrome

Symptoms: sufferers tend to believe that whatever they are told is not true, that 'it just can't be like that!', that something is too good to be true, too simple to be effective, absolutely impossible.

Let's get one thing straight: I will never ask you to take my word for anything; all I ask is that you simply try what I suggest. Others have done it before you, and their lives have been transformed as a result.

I'm not asking you to believe me I am asking you to try.

Let one dominant idea guide you as you work with this method: 'I have unlimited resources at my disposition.'

'I have unlimited resources.'

> **YOU'RE WORTH A HUNDRED TIMES MORE THAN YOU THINK**

Together we're going to take a look at these unlimited resources, and at the problems you encounter as you try to live well. You now have a guide at your disposal - this method - which will help you put certain techniques into action, techniques which arise spontaneously as we think and discover together.

Before going any further, take a short break. Read over what we've covered up to now, and make sure to underline anything that strikes you as important, if you haven't already done so.

WEEK 2 -- ADAPTING

All living creatures have to adapt to survive. Let's look at an example from nature.

If Arctic hares were white during the summer, they'd make perfect targets. That's why their coats turn rust brown in the spring. In winter they become completely white like snow, which makes them less vulnerable to predators. In other words, if they want to survive, Arctic hares must adapt to their surroundings.

If I dressed up in winter clothes during summer I'd suffocate. In the same way, if I wore light clothes in winter I'd probably get pneumonia and maybe even die.

So we're always adapting to the temperature of our environment. Soldiers are taught to become experts in the art of camouflage. If they don't adapt they will die. If they're not killed immediately, chances are they will be sooner or later.

Now, why do people get depressed? Because they are unable to adapt to other people, to events, situations, to problems that arise, and so on.

Let's look at a few examples.

Jules, an excellent worker, is promoted to foreman. But Jules feels intimidated by his fellow workers. He's afraid to give them orders; he soon becomes tense, nervous and irritable, because he feels he can't cope with his new position. His wife and friends don't know what to do. After two months of insomnia and bad digestion he's on the point of having a nervous breakdown. Can you indicate the reason?

Mrs L was happy in her role of mother and housewife; she had a lot of friends who admired and respected her. Her husband, a bank director, was suddenly transferred to the other end of the country. Mrs L. grew bored in the new city; she couldn't seem to make any friends, she didn't know what to do with herself, slept badly at night, and ended up feeling depressed and crying for no apparent reason. Can you guess why?

Mr D was very happy living with his wife and beautiful four-year-old son. But then his wife got pregnant again. Tragedy struck and she died in childbirth, along with the infant. Mr D fell apart. He started drinking heavily, he'd break into tears at the mere sight of his son, he refused to see his friends, spoke only about his wife, hardly slept and lost a tremendous amount of weight. In the end he had to be placed under medical supervision. For what reason, do you think?

The answers, of course, are simple: Jules didn't know how to adapt to his new job; Mrs L didn't know how to adapt to the change of city, and Mr D didn't know how to adapt to the tragedy of his wife's death, I'm not saying it would have been easy for Jules or Mrs L, and especially for Mr D, to adapt to these events. No. But they all suffered because they didn't know how to adapt.

Before going any further I'd like you to stop for a moment and think about any people you may be having trouble adapting to.

Write down the names of anyone you are having trouble adapting to: your partner, for example, or your boss, your neighbor, one of your in-laws, a friend of your partner, a relative, one of your children or grandchildren, a colleague or a new manager at work.

Circumstance	Why

Would you like to know whether you have trouble adapting ?

Think about each of the following questions and answer as truthfully as you can.

- Do I feel uncomfortable when I'm introduced to someone I have never met before?
- Do I like participating in new group situations? Meeting new people?
- Do I enjoy going to places alone, places where I know I'll meet people?
- Do I get upset if my partner or children get home late?
- Do I get worried easily?
- Am I afraid of seeing my children grow up?
- Do I long for the 'good old days'?

- Do I have trouble coping with all the changes in our fast-paced world (work, school, fashion, relationships)?
- Do I feel comfortable with my work?
- Do I get upset if dinner isn't ready on time, if the kids cry, if my car doesn't start, if something unexpected happens?
- Can I remember names easily?
- Do I trust people easily?
- Do I often bicker with my family or with people I know?

Then write down why. Write whatever comes into your head, just let your thoughts flow (because she thinks she's smarter than I am, because he can get me fired, because she's always so well dressed, because I'm afraid of making a fool of myself in front of him, because he's got ten times more money than I have, because she makes me feel so fat, because I feel uncomfortable when I'm with her, because I can't figure him out, because he gets angry all the time).

Name	Why

You can also have problems adapting to events or unexpected situations. Think about the kinds of situations you'd prefer to avoid, and write them down. Then write down why you want to avoid them. (For example: Frankly, I don't know what would happen to me if I lost my father. I'd probably have a nervous breakdown... If I was ever offered another job I don't know what I'd do, moving somewhere else and starting over from scratch ... I don't look forward to seeing my children grow up and become teenagers ... Start my own business? Never! It's just too risky.)

Situation	Why

And finally, we can even have problems adapting to ourselves. Everyone has something they don't like about themselves. Write down the things that bother you about yourself, and explain why -not enough education, too fat, bad dresser, unattractive, bad speller-anything that makes you say:

- Ah, if only I'd stayed in school longer!
- Ah, if only I were ten years younger!
- Ah, if only I were always sure of myself, like my friend so and so.

Now make a kind of inventory of yourself and your life.

Are you satisfied with:

Your health?

[]Yes []No []I can do something about it []I can't do anything about it

Your education?

[]Yes []No []I can do something about it []I can't do anything about it

Your gender?

[]Yes []No []I can do something about it []I can't do anything about it

Your physical appearance?

[]Yes []No []I can do something about it []I can't do anything about it

Your job?

[]Yes []No []I can do something about it []I can't do anything about it

Your family?

[]Yes []No []I can do something about it []I can't do anything about it

Your friends?

[]Yes []No []I can do something about it []I can't do anything about it

The town you live in?

[]Yes []No []I can do something about it []I can't do anything about it

Your income?

[]Yes []No []I can do something about it []I can't do anything about it

Your house?

[]Yes []No []I can do something about it []I can't do anything about it

Your (note any other important factors):

[]Yes []No []I can do something about it []I can't do anything about it

[]Yes []No []I can do something about it []I can't do anything about it

In the cases where you aren't satisfied and think you can do something about it, what changes would you like to make? Indicate the things you are going to do to make these changes.

What I want to change	What I have to do

I hope you know yourself a little better now: who you are, what you have, what can make you uncomfortable, what frightens you. Now let's look at what adapting consists of.

- If I have the talent to direct a company yet find myself doing some uninteresting manual job, am I adapting?
- If I only have the talent to be a worker and suddenly get promoted to foreman, am I adapting?
- If I have to visit someone and I'm afraid of making a bad impression, am I adapting?
- If I have to appear on television and I'm afraid of being nervous, am I adapting?
- If I have to go to a formal dinner and know nothing about the rules of etiquette, am I adapting?
- If I go to a party wearing casual clothes and find everyone else is dressed up, am I adapting?

You can see that in all the above situations you are unhappy because you haven't adapted well. Now try to describe, in your own words, what adapting means:

To be happy, to lead a rich and fulfilling lire, you must adapt, first to yourself and then to others. That is the basic condition for success. To start with you must accept yourself as you are, your physical appearance, your age, weight, height, education, job. But there's more to it than that.

Adapting means feeling ready for any situation

When you don't feel ready, when you don't feel up to a given situation, it means you haven't adapted.

These days adapting is a major problem for many people. Everything is going so fast! Modern life is just too full of stress. That's why so many modern illnesses are stress-related, caused by an inability to adapt: heart attacks, stomach ulcers, nervous breakdowns.

Why is it that some people adapt while others don't? First, let me say that everyone, even the most balanced, influential or famous people - everyone without exception - has, at some time or other, had problems adapting.

And whenever you have a problem adapting it's because you feel inferior. I'm not saying you have an inferiority complex, you just momentarily feel inferior, which isn't the same thing at all.

When you feel inferior you feel small or stupid or uncomfortable or inadequate. You may freeze up, or be unable to smile, or feel that you just want to disappear.

The sensation may last for a few seconds; sometimes it lasts for an entire evening ... or in some cases, for an entire lifetime!

Feelings of inferiority are part of human psychology. A very well-known German psychologist, Olivier Brachenfeld, spent his life studying inferiority. Here's what he has to say on the subject: 'The best way to fight inferiority is to cultivate the feeling of fraternity.'

In other words, if you feel unable to adapt it's because you feel inferior. And if you feel inferior it's simply because you are not fraternizing with the person who is making you feel uncomfortable. You feel inferior to that person, inferior to the task at hand, you feel 'small'.

Cultivating a sense of fraternity or kinship with others helps us adapt to people we meet. Now take a moment to write down a few ways that you think will help you express this sense of fraternity with others in your everyday life.

We have used the science of psychology to discover why you may have trouble adapting to others, and how to overcome the problem. What do you have to do to adapt to new or unexpected situations? The answer lies in a branch o psychology called 'characterology', the study of character.

As you may know, characterology divides people into eight main character types: passionate, choleric, phlegmatic, sanguine, nervous, sentimental, apathetic and amorphous.

Nervous, sentimental, apathetic and amorphous people adapt badly. They lack the ability to act.

Passionate, choleric, phlegmatic and sanguine types adapt well. They are more active.

But the ability to act can be developed, just like a muscle. So if you say, I'm not the type of person who adapts well!' you may be right, but a better way of putting it would be to say, 'If I have trouble adapting, it's because I'm not active enough.'

You therefore have to increase your level of activity in order to adapt more easily to the world around you.

But it isn't enough to know what you have to do to adapt better, to feel able to cope. You also have to want to do it. So from now on, every time you are confronted with a situation you have trouble adapting to, think about these two points: fraternity and action.

Fraternity and action

Find something to do, take the first step, get up and approach people. If you're living through a difficult moment, try not to think about your discomfort. Instead, do something about it! Get your body involved and act. For example, do some deep breathing for a few moments, or force yourself to smile, or make sure your posture is good, or extend your hand to someone you don't know. Your heart will follow naturally, and a sense of friendship will grow inside you, real feelings generated and expressed by your smile and your welcoming approach to others. So try to adapt better by taking action each and every day: do things for people, offer to buy someone a coffee, call someone who would ordinarily intimidate you, and so on.

I'm not asking you to believe me. I'm just asking you to try.

Summary

1. We have to adapt in order to survive.

2. Adapting means feeling able to cope.

3. To adapt to people: fraternize.

4. To adapt to situations: act.

WEEK 3 -- SELF-CONFIDENCE

Last week you did some thinking about adapting, and discovered certain ways to develop your sense of fraternity and ability to take action in order to adapt better to people and situations. Then you tried to put these methods into action. Because the important thing isn't to know but to act.

Act.

If you take a long journey which you know will be full of obstacles, but which will eventually lead you to some incredible destination, you won't let the obstacles stop you. However, you'll have to see them in order to avoid them.

Perhaps you know some people who have already made the trip, and who have benefited immensely from it. They don't keep talking about the obstacles; instead, they talk about reaching their goal.

Now where exactly are you going? It would be a good idea to have a map, wouldn't it? A map that shows you the route you have to follow, and your destination point.

How long will your journey last? What is its purpose? What means of transportation are you going to use? What provisions should you take along with you? What are you going to need along the way?

Your destination'? A better, more fulfilling life, and the attainment of success. How long will it take? This journey lasts a lifetime. But this method is a giant first step towards feeling a lot better about yourself, and becoming a more self-fulfilled person; it will endow you with a sense of purpose, the will to continue making progress your whole life long.

What stops will you be making along the way? To get to your destination - 'success' - you have to pass through 9 major 'cities':

- self-confidence;
- positive mental orientation;
- commitment;
- enthusiasm;
- self-expression;
- suggestion;
- relaxation;
- aptitude for happiness;

- success.

So your map is a kind of stairway, with success at the top.

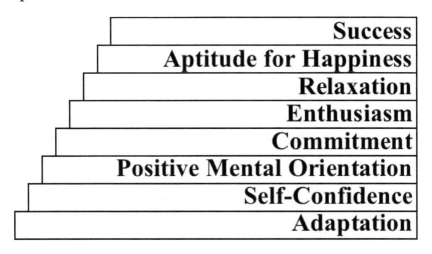

Success
Aptitude for Happiness
Relaxation
Enthusiasm
Commitment
Positive Mental Orientation
Self-Confidence
Adaptation

Now let's move up to the next step: Self-confidence.

Self-confidence is the basis of a strong and fully developed personality.

After some reflection on the subject of self-confidence we'll take a look at the means of transportation you can use to successfully complete this stage of your journey, and certain types of exercise will be indicated as you go along. Don't think that you can just sit back and wait for it all to happen after a few hours of reading!

You're going to have to roll up your sleeves and get to work, using your brain, your heart and your entire being.

Would you like to know whether you

are self confident?

Think about each of the following questions, and answer as honestly as you can:

- Do I blush easily?
- Do I get the feeling people enjoy seeing me wherever I go?
- Am I afraid of talking to people, getting mixed up, stuttering or making mistakes?
- Am I worried about other people's opinions?
- Do I often have thoughts like, 'I'm no good' or 'I'm so stupid!'?
- Do I feel comfortable enough to invite people into my home?
- Am I comfortable when speaking in front of people, at a party, a reception, a meeting?
- Do I enjoy speaking in public?
- Have I ever refused to join a group, or do some recruiting, or sell subscriptions or raffle tickets'?
- What social activities do I participate in?
- Do I prefer being alone or with other people?
- Am I afraid of what other people think about me?
- Am I afraid of other people making fun of me?
- Do people consider me tough, hard to get along with,

closed in'?

- Do the people around me, my partner, my children, my co-workers, tend to confide in me easily when they have problems?
- Am I capable of making fast decisions on my own?
- Do I tend to regret my decisions once they're made?

Having self-confidence means knowing what your capacities and limits are. You know how strong you are because you're not afraid to try things out, to see how much you can lift, how far you can run. But trying out your mental capacities can be a little frightening, because of the risk of failure this involves. In other words, we're afraid of ourselves. And yet we possess so many hidden possibilities, just waiting for a chance to reveal themselves. If we could only liberate those forces imprisoned inside us, we could show the world that we're worth a hundred times more than we think we are today.

How to develop your self-confidence

How do you know if you're confident or not? What signs should you look for in someone else to determine whether they are self-confident?

People who lack self-confidence show it in one of several ways.

- They may be shy and nervous, afraid to assume

responsibilities, afraid of the unknown, and have an almost obsessive need to feel secure (soliciting reassurance in all kinds of ways).

- They can also be short-tempered and insist on perfection (they'll make sure they do every little thing better than anyone else).
- They are very concerned about what others think about them
- They are rigid and stubborn, and find it very difficult to adroit that they're wrong.
- They make mountains out of molehills, are often rude and surly, and tend to overreact to any little thing.
- They exhibit altogether different symptoms: aggression can also be a sign of a lack of self-confidence. Unconfident people often depend on things like position, money, physical prowess or new cars to make themselves feel important.

People who cannot admire others also lack self-confidence. They are afraid that by praising others they will diminish their own worth.

Can someone be too self-confident? We meet people every day who we could say are suffering from a superiority complex. But there's no such thing as a superiority complex! These people really feet inferior, and try to disguise their fears by being arrogant and overbearing.

Never forget that people who are really self-confident are never autocratic or authoritarian. They don't have to be the leader of the gang all the time, because they have enough confidence in themselves to be able to have confidence in others, creating an aura of harmony wherever they go.

It is that kind of self-confidence that we're going to try and develop throughout these chapters, and for the rest of out lives.

A driving license to steer your life towards success

At first glance it may seem easy to acquire self-confidence. But things like natural laziness, our fear of the unknown and of making a real effort, our ingrained habits and lack of training, all represent serious obstacles along the way. Yet obstacles are not necessarily frightening; they can also be seen as signs, warning us to take precautions and avoid being caught unawares.

Say you hop into your car and set off on a long journey which you know will be full of obstacles. What's the first precaution you take before leaving? You have your car checked out thoroughly, of course: tires, transmission, brakes.

Our mental vehicle is often in pretty bad shape: we steer our way through life in a defective machine. You accept the fact that you need a license to drive a car, so why not get a 'person license' and learn how to direct your life? Unfortunately, neither school nor lire experience can provide you with such a license.

Let's have a little fun with the example of the car (we tend to remember things a lot longer if we're having fun when we learn them). We're going to talk about some simple truths, truths we tend to forget precisely because they are so simple.

Is our motor in good condition? Are all our springs and gears working properly? I'm going to describe a few types of behavior, and if you happen to recognize yourself in any of them, be kind enough to have a good laugh about it, would you?

Do you recognize yourself in any of these portraits?

Some people go through life with a 'dead battery', so to speak. They leave their headlights on needlessly. In the weeks that follow you're going to learn how to recharge your battery through relaxation, and how to avoid wasting energy

Some people go through life without any fuel! They're always running to family or friends, to bars and restaurants to 'tank up' and get 'turned on'. They don't have the enthusiasm it takes to make progress. They are completely dependent on others.

Some people have a defective transmission. They go into reverse when they should be going forward, and usually end up 'running around in circles'. We should be using our mental gearbox to adapt ourselves to the pace of circumstance around us, but it so often happens that we plough ahead when we should be idling in neutral.

How many times has your steering malfunctioned, so that you turned left when you should have turned right? You don't even know how to control your own thoughts! You want success, but you keep steering yourself in ways that lead to failure. You want to be healthy, yet you do things that make you ill. You want to be able to talk to your children, but you cut them off from yourself. Your steering is out of order. Starting in the next lesson we'll be working on mastering the art of steering your life - in other words, controlling your thoughts.

Some people have enormous inner strength, as if they were 'turbo-charged' with energy, and yet they express themselves as if they were powered by a two-stroke lawn mower engine. They have the talent to be national leaders, and yet they vegetate, moving from one uninteresting job to another. On the other hand, some people really do have two-cylinder engines, yet they act as if they were Rolls-Royces. Such people pretend to be someone they aren't, suffering from exaggerated superiority complexes. What you're going to team is how to move along at your own pace, without dragging your feet or burning your engine.

Some people don't know how to brake or accelerate properly: they try to pretend they're better than they really are, and do not know how to control their sensitivity and nerves. If they see an obstacle in front of them they don't know how to put on the brakes, and when they should forge ahead they don't have the courage to press on the accelerator.

Some people don't even know where they're headed; they just keep going straight ahead, or even worse, let chance steer them where it will. They have no goals, no ideals; they go through life without asking any questions, simply because they exist. These are the type of people who take care of the body of their car, always making sure it looks good, and forget about keeping the motor in good shape. They are preoccupied with material comforts, money, rich food, luxurious houses or boats. But they remain poor in terms of personality, and are never really happy. They set aside enough money every month to pay the rent, heating, telephone, food, entertainment and so on, but completely forget about their personal development.

Learning to live better, to be happier and to develop your self-esteem has no price. Improving yourself, investing time and money in yourself is the best investment you can make. Because what you add to your personality can never be taken away from you.

I have just described a few personality types, and I am fairly certain you recognized yourself in one or another of them. Stop for a moment and take the time to indicate which of these personality types you belong to:

You may have recognized something of yourself in a few of the examples. Your lack of self-confidence may be due to a number of factors. You must work on these points and develop your self-confidence, until you become a motorist who has complete confidence in his/her vehicle: tires, motor, transmission, battery. If any one of these elements is not up to par, your self-confidence will surfer.

Self-confidence is the result of a number of factors. As you resolve your problems in the areas of adaptation, self-expression, relaxation, controlling your thoughts and feelings, mastering your nerves, you will feel your self-confidence grow.

Your self-confidence grows in proportion to your assurance that your 'vehicle' is running smoothly, that your motor is in good shape and you are in full control of yourself.

Break out of the vicious circle

But how can you gain such control? What do you have

to do to become self-confident? Well, you will succeed by developing the following factors: enthusiasm, the ability to relax, the ability to adapt, controlling your thoughts, mastering your feelings, and learning to express your personality.

Now, how should you go about doing this? Aren't we caught in some kind of vicious circle here - you lack self-confidence, therefore you lack enthusiasm, so how can you develop enthusiasm in order to have more self-confidence? No. There is a way out, a very simple way, actually so simple that I hesitate to tell you what it is. Because people tend to believe only in complicated solutions, it's like a deeply ingrained habit!

A very simple way to master your personality

To master your personality you first have to get your muscles to do what you want. You have to act on your body, on your exterior attitudes first. You have to work through the vehicle of your body. Now, you can't control all the muscles in your body, but there are some that you can control. Your diaphragm, for example, and through your diaphragm your breathing. This is a very simple, and yet extremely important point: you can control your breathing. And breathing is the basis of self-control.

To breathe properly you have to feel good, you have to be optimistic and joyous. But the opposite is also true: simply by breathing properly you can get yourself into a good mood and feel more optimistic and joyous. Breathing purifies your body. It expels carbon dioxide and stimulates your glands, promoting good health. Your lungs are connected to all other organs, and every time you stimulate your lungs you also stimulate all your other organs, causing them to function better. Now I can hear you saying, 'But I knew that already!' I'm not in the least surprised. But the important thing is not knowing, it's doing. It is putting into practice what you already know.

Your inner world is expressed through your exterior appearance

Sound too simple? Do you have any doubts? Well, just get up and take a look in a mirror. What do you see? A person who looks optimistic? Happy? A person who exudes self-confidence? Or someone who is angry, worried or depressed?

Your face and outward attitudes are the mirrors of your soul. They are the physical manifestations of your inner world. Would you like to be angry? All you have to do is adopt an aggressive attitude, clench your fists, cross your arms, grate your teeth...

Would you like to be optimistic? Happy? Would you like to be self-confident? Feel comfortable? Well adapted to life? Enthusiastic? Well, just put on a big smile, straighten your back, breathe properly, look people in the eye, stand tall ... and above all, above all, don't wait until you feel happy to stall!

All this just to make you think about something that is very simple and yet so easy to forget: your body influences your mind, and your mind influences your body.

Whatever you think is expressed through your body.

That's why breathing is so important. It is the basis of controlling your body.

Like mechanics in a garage, we have to work on our vehicle in order to get it to perform well. That's right, I said work! Because it's not what you read or hear that is going to change anything, it's what you do.

During the course of these lessons you'll be doing various relaxation and mental exercises, complimented by additional reading, and very soon you'll be taking some 'mental sampling' and doing exercises to get your muscles into shape. But we have to start at the beginning, with breathing.

This week's exercises

How can you make your body a more manageable

instrument of self-expression? Through relaxation exercises. And in order to relax you have to learn to breathe properly, and assume the correct posture by imagining that you're floating on the surface of a body of water.

Starting today, every day, morning and night, stretch out on your back and take the time to do ten deep breathing exercises. And by deep breathing I don't mean inflating your chest and trying to look like Rambo! No. Deep breathing means full abdominal breathing. You place a hand on your stomach and feel it rising first, and then you feel the air filling your lungs. And when you've inhaled as much as you can ... you release the air slowly, emptying your lungs, and finally feel your stomach contracting (try to keep a window open as you do this exercise).

Then, whenever you feel tired, nervous or overworked during the course of a day, instead of lighting up a cigarette or drinking a glass of alcohol, or cup of coffee, stretch out on your back and take the time to do some deep breathing.

These preliminary exercises are very important. Make sure you do them every day, not all at once just to get them out of the way, but conscientiously, morning and night.

Don't forget that developing self-confidence requires constant and daily work on yourself. You have to keep a close watch on your exterior attitudes and modify them so that your interior eventually assumes the shape you want. And to do that, you have to start at the beginning - with breathing.

I can assure you that in a very short time you'll be feeling so much better you'll say, 'Hum! This is just like one of Grandma's cures - the simpler it is, the better it works!'

Summary

1. Self-confidence is the basis of a happy personality.

2. Being self-confident means knowing your capacities, limits and possibilities.

3. Acquiring self-confidence is the result of daily work in areas like adapting, relaxation, controlling your thoughts and feelings, self-expression.

4. To acquire more self-confidence you have to modify your exterior attitudes.

5. To modify your exterior attitudes, you have to start by controlling your breathing, which is the only bodily function you have direct control over.

WEEK 4 -- POSITIVE MENTAL ORIENTATION

Well, a week has gone by during which you've benefited from the relaxing effects of controlled breathing. You did your breathing exercises conscientiously and faithfully, I'm sure, and I want to congratulate you. That's right, congratulations! The things I asked you to do were all very simple and yet extremely important: they are the basis of our re-education program.

Now I'd like you to think about what it is that makes people healthy or sick, successful or besieged by problems, happy or unhappy. I'd like to talk about steering your 'vehicle', about controlling your thoughts - in other words, about positive mental orientation.

What is positive mental orientation? Well, it's simply the opposite of negative mental orientation!

What do you see in this drawing?

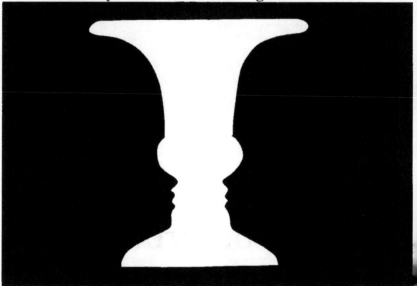

If you look at the dark part, you see two heads; if you look at the light part you see a vase. Your existence is like this drawing: you can see the light or the dark side of things. It's up to you, and you alone, to decide.

The world is a mirror which reflects your smile or your frown

We're going to think about the way we see the world, the people and events around us: too often we see them in a negative light. We forget that the world is a mirror which reflects our smiles or our frowns.

This lesson is of capital importance, because the way

you steer your vehicle is what causes accidents or gets you where you want to go. It is essential to know how to steer, how to orient yourself.

This fact is so important, and yet it is so neglected that our century has become plagued by problems of the mind. And I'm not just talking about mental illness. There is also a host of stress-related physical conditions. It's amazing when you consider that although human beings control the world, they don't know how to control their own thoughts!

Do you exhibit any of these symptoms of negative mental orientation?

1.　　A mania for spreading bad news: are you the first to inform others of death, illness, financial problems, personal scandal, theft? How your life could change for the better if you made a point of spreading only good news!

2.　　A mania for gossiping: 'I don't want to say anything bad about her, but I'm telling you, the way she's been behaving with her husband, I'm not surprised things turned out badly...'

'I always knew he'd end up being unfaithful to her, the way he flirts around all the time...'

'Did you hear about Mrs X's daughter? She's pregnant...'

Do you spend hours on the phone, gossiping about

others, sticking your nose into other people's business, criticizing Mrs X for the way she raises her children, or Mr Y for going out too much?

3.   Negative mental orientation creates a taste for the morbid, perverse or sensational: just look at the plethora of tabloid newspapers, with circulations running into hundreds of thousands, full of scandals of the rich and famous, horrible accidents, crimes, birth defects, and so on.

4.   A perverse need to always blame and belittle others: 'Mr X is doing well? Well, maybe, but I'm sure he's got something going with his secretary...

'You think he's a good speaker? Bah! He sounds like a drunk to me . . .

'They may have a nice house, but everything they own is mortgaged to the hilt.. '

'You liked the play? Well, it was all right, but the seats were so uncomfortable...'

'You think he's a good doctor? Well, he should be, considering what he gets paid!'

5.   Pessimism, an insatiable curiosity about others' weaknesses, constant worry, a tendency to overdramatize, and so on, are more manifestations of negative mental orientation. Here are a few examples:

How many women, waiting for their husbands, who happen to be running late, to get home from work, immediately envision the worst, imagine him lying in a ditch somewhere, in a pool of blood, his car a total wreck, calling out for help before taking a last, dying breath?

How many people refuse a promotion: 'Foreman? No way! Everyone hates the foreman.'

Me? Do some volunteer work? Never! I don't need the headaches!'

It's spring, the kids are going to get sick again.'

Such people are afraid of almost everything: afraid of getting sick, afraid of losing money, afraid of what others might say about them, afraid of what others think: they are afraid of affirming themselves, and they are even afraid of being themselves!

Other manifestations of negative mental orientation

Negative mental orientation shows up in language, attitudes and behavior.

Language

- Don't touch that!
- Don't do that!
- Don't move!
- You're late again!
- You'll never get your life together!

- You can't sit still for two minutes!

- What do you think about her? She's not bad!

- What's the weather like? It's not bad!

- What do you think? It's not so bad!

- How are you? Not too bad!

Attitudes

- Young people today are so stupid!

- Things are going too well. It'll never last!

- I feel too good. Something terrible's going to happen, I know it!

- I knew it. He hasn't done anything about it for weeks.

- I feel like I'm going to have a tummy upset

- Men are all the same!

- Life is so hard, isn't it?

- It's easy for you to talk, you don't have a 12-year-old child to worry about.

Behavior

- Being suspicious of compliments because you think people are hiding something.

- Not daring to give advice or state your opinions about anything.

We can sometimes be negative even when we're complimenting someone:

- Well, for once you managed to cook something that

tastes good!

- You finally make an effort, my boy, and you come in second!

- I didn't think you had it in you to do something like this!

- Don't tell me you finally had enough guts to ask for a raise!

- A child proudly brings a painting to show Mother, and all she can say is, 'Look at you, your hands are filthy and you've got stains all over your clothes!'

- A husband notices his wife's new dress, and the house all tidied up, and says, 'God, it smells awful in here! What, did you wax the floors again?' Instead of commenting on the clean floors, all he can do is smell the wax.

We can also be negative in the way we receive compliments:

- Someone says they like the hat we're wearing and we say, 'Oh that old thing! I've had it for two years.'

- 'What a pretty bracelet you have.'

- 'Oh well, it's not real gold.'

- Your husband is so charming.'

- 'Yeah, when he's with company.'

Almost everyone has received a negative education, which follows us around like a shadow. We have been taught to be apprehensive about sexuality; love is negative; the state of the country is always negative. So it shouldn't surprise us when we discover we are negative without even knowing it. And that is precisely the crux of the problem: we are negative, and we don't even know it! Negative thought patterns impregnate our entire life, or family, the education of our children, our social life, our health, our entire existence. We have been poisoned without being aware of it! Education is the cause of our negative way of thinking. Now it's up to us, as adults, to re-educate ourselves and orient our thoughts in a positive way.

The education you provide for yourself

There are two kinds of education, the kind you receive from others, and the kind you give yourself.

You don't need to take a course in psychology to understand the importance of positive mental orientation, to experience the joy that comes from actions which are done in a positive frame of mind. You know that sick people who have a positive outlook get better faster than those who are irritable and always complaining about how they feel. You know that people who are always thinking dark thoughts end up depressed; you know that stomach ulcers are caused by stress, and insomnia by worry.

So for the sake of our health and happiness, we

absolutely must acquire a more positive outlook on life.

Would you like to know whether or not you have a positive mental orientation?

Think about the following questions and answer as truthfully as you can:

[] When I talk to my children, do I often say things like, 'Don't touch!' or 'Don't do that!' or 'Keep quiet!' or 'Don't get dirty!' or 'Hurry up!'?

[] Do I tend to compliment my partner, my children, my colleagues?

[] Do I enjoy receiving compliments, or am I suspicious about people's underlying motives'?.

[] Do I worry easily?

[] Do I surfer from 'stage fright'? Am I afraid that I'll make a fool of myself in front of others?

[] Do I often feel depressed?

[] Do I sleep well?

[] Do I enjoy reading sensational tabloids or magazines?

[] Do I like horror movies or movies that are very violent?

[] Do I tend to enjoy spreading bad news?

[] Do I have any specific fears: fear of being robbed, of tire, cancer, death, thunder, getting sick, fainting?

[]   Am I usually in a good mood?

[]   Do I often find myself humming or singing a tune?

[]   Do I like telling stories to children?

[]   Do I tend to see the bright side of things naturally and easily?

[]   Do I often talk about sickness, accidents, or other depressing or sad events?

[]   Do I live, or spend a lot of time with sad or nervous people?

Negative mental orientation can often be detected in the way we speak, our attitudes and our behavior. Indicate the ways in which you think you exhibit your negative mental orientation, and what you can do to make your way of speaking, your attitudes and behavior more positive:

You may be thinking that it's all very well to be positive, but that optimists have just as much chance of being wrong as pessimists. That's true, but optimists are still much happier than pessimists. Because happiness does not depend on other people, on material things or events. No. You create or destroy your own happiness, according to the way you think. Having a positive orientation is like dialing the right telephone number: you get through to the person you're trying to reach a lot faster than if you just dial a number at random, or dial the Wrong number on purpose!

Control the effects events have on you

Of course, you often cannot control events themselves. But what you can and should control are the effects events have on you. You may lose a loved one, your job, your money, even one of your children, but that's still no reason to have a nervous breakdown. And the encouraging thing is that adopting a positive mental orientation is something that can be learned, just like learning a foreign language.

It's much easier to learn a foreign language if you live in a country where that language is spoken. The same goes for positive mental orientation. If you are surrounded by positive people, it's a lot easier to learn how to control yourself and how to maintain a positive outlook. Creating a positive atmosphere for your children is one of the best things you can do for them.

Finally, you should not keep comparing yourself to others, but rather to yourself: compare what you were not so long ago to what you are now, to what you are in the process of becoming, to the person you'd like to be. To do this you have to examine the way you act during the course of a day, at work, with your family, with friends. Note down your weak points, and also what you are going to do to try and improve. Make a careful analysis of your behavior every day.

Some examples of positive mental orientation

Here are a few more examples of a life lived with a positive mental orientation:

- talking to your children calmly instead of shouting at them all the time;
- turning off the TV or radio (not in the middle of a program, which may upset others);
- replacing negative speech patterns with positive ones; for example, saying in calm voice, 'Would you mind speaking a little more softly, dear,' instead of screaming, 'Will you stop shouting!' · never saying negative things about children when they are present, things like, 'He's so shy, he gets all tongue-tied for nothing,' or 'This one will never amount to much.'
- praising your children, your partner or colleagues for a job well done;
- saying 'please' and 'thank you';
- making an effort to compliment others;
- finding something positive to say when things are going badly;
- smiling for at least rive minutes every day, no matter what happens.

Smile and the world will smile with you.

Changing the way you think changes your entire being.

Action gets rid of tension

Sometimes when you feel nervous or worried or fearful it's because you are inactive. As soon as you feel one or another of these uncomfortable sensations, which usually precede taking action, you should be on your guard. They don't necessarily mean that the action you are about to undertake is beyond your capacities. They just mean that your organism is getting ready to make some kind of unusual effort.

If you have some difficult task to perform, an important phone call to make or a problem to resolve, remember that you won't be able to feel completely relaxed until you've accomplished what you have to do. If you hesitate, you burn up energy needlessly. So pick up the telephone and make your call; the test will take care of itself. Do whatever it is you have to do, and never procrastinate.

This doesn't mean you shouldn't think before you act and just plunge ahead unprepared. But once you are prepared, you should be confident that you have the strength required to do what has to be done. Tell yourself that whatever you can imagine you can do. To succeed you have to aim high, think big and be ambitious. How can you accomplish anything if you keep on thinking things like:

- I'll never be able to do it!'
- 'It's too much of a risk for me to take. I haven't got what it takes.'

Therefore, since action frees you from stress, whenever you feel tired, nervous, tense or worried, instead of brooding do some breathing exercises, or go jogging, jump up and down, sing -anything that gets you moving - and then act!

Sending thank-you notes

Would you like to develop a simple habit of positive mental orientation? Try sending thank-you notes or emails to people, with the aim of making life a little more pleasant for them, helping people discover positive values which they often overlook.

The simple habit teaches you to look for the bright side of events and of the people around you. You will soon see that systematically seeking out the good, the positive side of things, will transform your way of thinking. At first you'll show your thanks for the good things people usually do, and then you'll start discovering good things which you never noticed before.

Thank-you notes are sent, often unsigned, to friends

or acquaintances. The reasons for thanking someone are infinite:

- Thank you for your patience the other day.
- The meal you made for us last weekend was absolutely delicious!

Choose someone you'd like to thank right now, and write them a little note or send an email. Do this each and every day and you'll soon be so preoccupied with searching for the good things people do that you'll completely stop being critical. Seeing life through a pair of rose-colored glasses, you say? Well, what if it is? As long as it makes you a happier person!

Now let's look at another exercise, which has an almost magical effect in keeping you in top shape, starting your day on a positive note, getting rid of fatigue and establishing your positive orientation for the rest of the day.

Take a cold shower every morning

I'd like to talk about the benefits of taking a cold morning shower. Come on, don't grit your teeth! Smile! That's right. Now let me explain.

Taking a cold morning shower is such a simple and beneficial exercise. You may have to get up a few minutes earlier, but after a few weeks of faithful adherence to this you'll feel transformed, and will never want to give it up.

You'll be amazed at how good you feel after a cold shower, with the blood pumping through your veins and your skin invigorated and breathing as it should.

Can you understand that your positive mental orientation bas to begin as soon as you get out of bed? If you start by gritting your teeth and shivering even before you get under the shower, the exercise will be torture for you. To avoid this start by drinking a large glass of cold water, very slowly, and think about the benefits a cold shower will provide throughout the test of the day, getting you into top shape. Then take a deep breath, turn on the shower and let the water splash over your feet and legs. After a few seconds of this, step under the jet of water and stay there for between fifteen seconds and two minutes.

... and a warm evening shower

Do the same thing at night using warm water, since this will prepare you for sleep.

Don't believe anyone who tells you that cold showers are bad for your health, or that they can induce a chill or cause you to catch cold. On the contrary, most people who were used to catching colds all winter long have cured themselves by taking cold showers, which increase your resistance to cold. As for lukewarm showers before bedtime, there's nothing better for getting rid of stress-related fatigue and minor discomforts.

Now that you have firmly decided to take a cold shower every morning, you can start gradually. First take a lukewarm shower, and then slowly shut the hot water off while opening the cold water. This will help you acclimatize to your cold shower, rapidly and without any discomfort.

After your cold shower tub your entire body rigorously with a towel. This will invigorate your entire system. Then stretch out on your back, on a carpet or a hard bed, and do your deep breathing exercises. These exercises will get your day off to a fine start. You'll feel full of vigor and zest, almost as if you've been reborn!

Remember that you always start with your body when you're trying to improve your mind. And also remember that if you cheat on your cold shower, you're going to cheat on other things as well.

Health, happiness, love of life ... all these things are states of mind: tell yourself that from now on you are going to orient yourself towards everything that is positive. Starting tomorrow, on to the moment you get up, everything you do will be geared towards making you a happier person. Make a conscious effort to positive mental orientation for an entire week. And you will soon start wondering whether the world around you has changed, because inside you the world will.

Summary

- The world is a mirror which reflects your smile or your frown.

- In order to orient your mind in a positive way, you first have to realize your own negative orientation.

- We cannot control events, but we can control the way events affect us.

- Happiness does not depend on other people, material things or events. It depends on yourself, and the orientation you give your life.

- Changing the way you think means changing who you are.

- Smile and the world will smile with you!

WEEK 5 -- COMMITMENT

Now that you are able to orient yourself more positively we're going to try and understand one of the fundamental exercises of personal development. The exercise has a rather strange name: mental sampling. But it's really very simple.

We have already seen how we alone are responsible for our own happiness. We have seen how many of our actions in the past tended to be negative. We've realized how much time we've wasted taking care of everything except ourselves, so it's time for a change!

Now, if a doctor wants to know the hemoglobin count in your blood, for example, he's not going to drain all the blood out of your system into a bucket and study it! He'll get a lab to take a small blood sample, and from the sample he can see if you're anemic, or if you lack certain essential minerals or vitamins. If there is a problem, he will prescribe the appropriate medication, and then take another blood sample later on to see if there has been an improvement.

A sample of our behavior

We're going to do much the same thing here, and take a small sample of our behavior.

A person's fist, for example, is a kind of sample: you can see a person's personality in the way they make a fist. A person's eyes are another indicator: if someone doesn't look at you when they're talking to you, but keeps shifting their gaze or staring at the floor, then you can assume that the person is nervous or intimidated.

Posture is a good indicator of someone's personality. Ask yourself if you have the same posture when you're about to leave for a holiday as you do when you're in a meeting with your boss.

Have you noticed that just by listening to someone's voice on the telephone you can tell if that person is angry, happy, tired? You can tell a person's sex, age or country of origin just from their voice. So voice quality is a concentrated sample of who a person is, what their state of mind is, and so on.

Now, you want to change your entire life, not just the

surface aspects. You want to be more self-confident. You want to be in control, not only on those rare occasions when you have to speak in public, but in your everyday life, in your relations with your partner, your friends, your children, your family. Isn't that what you want?

'Extrapolating' out lives

But you also understand that it would be impossible to keep a record of everything you do or say all day long in order to find out whether or not you are applying your discoveries in personal development properly, just as it would be impossible for a doctor to drain all the blood out of your systems to find out what's wrong with you. What you can do is take a small slice of your life, say two minutes, as a sample, and from that detect what is right or wrong with your lire as a whole. This is called 'extrapolating': from one or a number of small samples you can tell what the bigger picture is like.

By taking a mental sample, we can see what aspects of out personality could be changed. Then we can prescribe an appropriate form of 'mental medication'. Here's a concrete example of how I look a mental sample and made a commitment to improve the faults I detected:

'I realize that my life is mediocre (compared to what it could be), that -------- has been bothering me for a long time now, that I absolutely must do something about it, and that I am going to take action immediately. I have taken a sample of my life, and here's how I feel:

'I've had enough of being afraid of everything, enough of being nervous. I will not tolerate this lack of communication with my children, or the anxiety I feel all the time. I'm through with suffering for no reason.

'From now on I will act like an adult. I am going to change. The people around me will not see me acting like a child who does everything he's told to do, but like a mature person who is in control of his life. Yes, all that is going to change, starting right now!'

Today, I decide to control my life instead of being directed by outside events. I commit myself to be the captain of my life and the master of my destiny in order to achieve success.

As you see, it took just one short minute to mobilize my mind against my pitiful mediocrity. The first thing you have to do is deal with what is bothering you. Then you make a decision to improve the situation. You commit yourself, through the feelings you express, and with the knowledge that you have the strength to take control of your life. If, in only one minute, I was able to act with so much force, then it means I do have the strength I need to make a change

If only . . .

If, on the contrary, I'd said: "Oh, I'm so tired of my mediocrity. I'm fed up with being so timid all the time, tired of being tired! If only I could, I'd love to change my life... I'd love to do such and such, if only I could..." then my attitude would have been one of defeat and indecision. Of course, if that kind of attitude only lasts a minute it wouldn't be so bad. But add up all the minutes I feel like that during the course of a day, and I come out looking like putty, on the point of having a nervous breakdown.

Commitment feeds on action

Mental illness, or "burn-out", is common these days. Nobody wants to have a breakdown, yet many people do. Therefore, you must take steps to protect yourself: first react, and then make a decision to act, to take control of your lire, at whatever cost. React, then act.

React, then act

Now, it's all very well to say that you've decided to change your lire, to be a mature adult, a happy person. But nothing changes until you start taking action.

To be certain about a feeling, about something you know, you have to be able to express it. For example, it's easy to say that I speak a foreign language, that a lot of people speak foreign languages, and so on. But ifs only by opening my mouth and actually speaking the language, and having people understand me, that I'm really sure I can speak that language. In other words, I have to demonstrate, both to myself and to others, that I can do what I say I can.

How to overcome paralysis

That's right, people who are incapable of expressing what they feel, incapable of revealing their enthusiasm and love, suffer as much as someone who can't walk because their legs are paralyzed. It's as painful to be paralyzed by an incapacity to react as it is to be unable to walk. And it's against this kind of paralysis that we'll be working together, using our mental samples as guides.

Remember, each human being is a whole person. They are a completely unique whole composed of a body, mind and spirit. So, it follows that the body, mind and spirit all influence and have an effect on one another. You know that if you have a headache you'll have a hard time concentrating, that suffering from an emotional heartache affects your appetite, that a sick person in good spirits recovers faster than someone who is depressed.

Human beings form a whole. A person who can't keep his house in order will also have a disorganized mind. A timid, introverted, closed woman will dress in pale, faded colors. A man who is oppressed by worry and anxiety will walk with stooped shoulders, all hunched up.

Because of this reciprocal influence of body and mind, anything that affects your body will also have an effect on your mind, and anything that affects your mind will have its physical repercussions. For example, anger translates into characteristic physical attitudes: tense body, clenched fists, accelerated heartbeat, frowning.

How to act on yourself

If you want to take action and change yourself it is best to begin with your body. You can start with your muscles, since you have direct control over them. Command your right leg to lift up off the ground and it will do so. On the other hand, you can't just tell your shyness to go away and expect it to obey. It is only through your muscles that you have direct control over yourself. What happens when you act on your muscles? Well, your actions are going to have an effect on your mind as well. Do you remember what we said in the last chapter? 'People who can't control their bodies can't control their thoughts.' I can't repeat this often enough.

This is a simple truth which we tend to forget in out everyday lives, and we play tricks on ourselves without even knowing it. For example, you don't have to wait until you aren't angry any more to relax the muscles in your hands. Relax your clenched fists, take a few deep breaths, smile, let your arms hang loose by your sides ... the rest will follow naturally. This will be effective no matter how angry you are.

We're playing tricks on ourselves when we slump down in a chair and say something like, 'I'm exhausted!' By slumping in a chair, hanging your head and complaining, you assume the attitude of fatigue, and this will only make your body feel more tired.

Acting on your inner self

So you first have to act on your muscles, on your body, on your exterior self. Not as an end, but as a means of acting on your inner self. Have you noticed how people are often more confident when they're well groomed? A perfect example of the influence of outer appearance on a person's inner frame of mind!

Start with the outside. You don't put on a long face because you're suffering. When you put on a long face you allow yourself to be overcome by suffering. Lift the corners of your mouth into a smile, straighten your shoulders, hold your head high, breathe deeply, hum a tune and you'll soon feel great again! If you want to pray you adopt an attitude of prayer. If you want to work, you get into the appropriate position, and you'll soon feel like working.

Your exterior gestures and behavior condition the way you feel inside. If you feel anxious, calmly sit down or walk around, turn off your computer, your mobile phone, the TV or the radio, breathe deeply and, as if by magic, you'll start feeling better.

You cannot exert direct control over your feelings. Instead, you exert control over your muscles, causing them to relax. If you feel angry with someone, reach out and take their hand, smile or give them a hug, and your anger will soon dissolve, allowing your inner self to become more disposed to feelings of friendship and love.

You've been practicing conscious breathing for a few weeks now. You know that breathing is the only bodily function over which you have full control. You cannot control your digestion, but you can always lie down and prolong or shorten your breathing. Do you understand now why breathing exercises are so important for regaining your inner calm and relaxing?

The influence of the conscious on the unconscious

Our conscious and unconscious minds are in constant communication. You know that your conscious mind is responsible for everything that happens inside you which you are aware of. For example, you're conscious that you're sitting down at this moment, reading and thinking. Your unconscious (some prefer the term 'subconscious') is responsible for everything that happens in you that you are not aware of. For example, you may not be aware that you are reliving childhood memories, or an experience from your adolescence, or something that happened during the course of the day, at this very moment.

Your subconscious is like a video machine that is constantly turned on, recording everything that happens to you and storing it for ever. Remember that these two parts of your mind are in constant communication.

Time does not exist for the subconscious

Say, for example, that when I was young someone told me I was shy or stubborn or lazy. I was conscious of the statement at the moment it was made. Since then it has remained recorded in my subconscious mind. And if my subconscious has recorded many negative impressions of fear, feelings of inadequacy, failure, guilt and so on, they will continue to influence my present behavior, without my knowing it.

Positive things may have happened in the past. They may be things which I was conscious of at the time they occurred - a success I had when I was seven years old, another at nine years old, various academic achievements between the ages of ten and eighteen. These will remain recorded in my subconscious mind, and will be of enormous help in attaining my present goals and achieving success in my adult lire.

Do you understand the importance of a positive education? Children become what people suggest they are, communicated to them through all sorts of words and gestures. Young birds are taught to fly by their elders.

The subconscious can help ... or harm us

The subconscious can be a help, for example in the acquisition of new, positive habits. Think about when you learned to type or drive a car. In the beginning you were conscious of all your movements, it was your conscious mind which did everything. Then, as you became more familiar with the activities involved, the movements became easier until one fine day you round yourself typing or driving without even thinking about it - the skills involved were recorded in your subconscious, and were there to stay.

| competent - subconscious |
| competent - conscious |
| incompetent - conscious |
| inconscious - incompetent |

Stages of learning or changing a habit

Work first on a conscious level to acquire new habits. Then, once they are recorded in your subconscious mind, they become what we call 'second nature'. In other words, you first have to work on your body with your conscious mind in order to influence your inner self.

What is a commitment?

A commitment is reflected by some outward behavior. It can take many forms: giving someone an engagement ring or signing a contract or a check, for example; once signed, you cannot renege on that contract without causing trouble.

Do you want to know if you are really committed to changing your life? Think about the following questions and answer as truthfully as you can.

    []   Is it easy for me to offer someone advice?

    []   Am I afraid of other people's opinions?

    []   Do I enjoy taking on responsibilities?

    []   Do I seem like a leader?

    []   Do friends often consult me about their

problems?

[]   Do I enjoy group discussions?

[]   Do I exercise authority at home and at work?

[]   Am I afraid of arguing?

[]   Do I encourage my children and my partner to say what they think?

[]   Do I think that by assuming responsibility I risk being disliked?

[]   Do I want everyone around me to have the same opinions as I do?

[]   Am I able to make decisions on my own, without asking for advice from a lot of people?

You need to commit yourself to getting rid of your negativity, your tension and your anxiety. You want to commit yourself to taking control of your life and making it a success. Now, think about what has been bothering you and decide to act. So what are you going to do now?

You need to follow through this commitment to action. Whenever we give up or make excuses without a good reason, we harm ourselves because the subconscious records it as failure, and we end up hurting out self-esteem.

Self-confidence means respecting your commitments

Would you trust someone who doesn't keep their

word? Would you have confidence in someone you couldn't count on? If you don't keep your word to yourself, you will end up without confidence in yourself.

You need to develop your capacity to respect commitment, so start with little things which are easy to do. Here's an example:

A short relaxation exercise

Get comfortable in a chair or, if possible, stretch out on your back on the floor. Breathe deeply, imagining your breath reaching down into your feet, and then exhale completely. Breathe in deeply, imagining your breath reaching down into your legs, and exhale completely.

Breathe in deeply, imagining breath into your calves, and exhale completely. Into your thighs ... and exhale completely. Into your hips.., your waist.., your stomach ... your back. . up to your chest...your shoulders...your arms...your hands ..your neck ... your head ... your cheeks...

This exercise doesn't take much time, yet it IS extremely beneficial, and you will feel deeply relaxed.

I'd like you to commit yourself in everything you do. No dilly dallying, no moaning and groaning, just apply yourself to the task at hand, and don't think about anything except what you're doing. There's nothing more tiring than doing something while your mind is wandering elsewhere:

doing the dishes and thinking about the ironing, or trying to get some work done at the office while your mind worries about an upcoming meeting. It only makes your job twice as hard.

Continue doing all your other exercises faithfully, now that you've got into the habit. And don't forget to add the new breathing-relaxation exercise you've just learned.

Summary

1. Mental sampling is like taking a test sample of your behavior.

2. Mental sampling is based on the following principle: because there is a unity to the way human beings behave there is a constant interchange or influence of body on mind, conscious on subconscious.

3. The opposite is also true: mind influences body, and the subconscious influences the conscious mind.

4. Through mental sampling I can mobilize my entire being against the problems in my lire and decide to act in order to change, improve and take control of my life.

5. To effect changes in myself, I should always start by acting on my body.

6. Changing my face means changing who I am.

7. The importance of the subconscious: children become what adults suggest they become; children only imitate adults; it is through example that we can influence others.

8. Self-confidence is a result of respecting the commitments we make to ourselves ... and to others.

WEEK 6 -- ENTHUSIASM

Well, here we are, already halfway to our destination! Maybe we should stop for a few minutes and take a look back at what we've already covered.

Since the start of the method you've been setting the foundations for change in your life, and trying out certain techniques to make your life more of a success. We set up a plan of action for overcoming nervousness, improving the way you express yourself, maintaining a positive mental attitude, and learning to adapt. Then you made a commitment to take control of your life, thereby increasing your self-confidence and making you a more fulfilled person.

You hardly learned anything new, but you now realize that the important thing is not knowing but taking action.

Today we're going to be talking about a very

important point, important not only for this method but for life in general. The point in question is enthusiasm.

You already know that if you are oriented towards health, beauty, success and happiness, you will experience health, beauty, success and happiness. You have understood that it is you and you alone who control your destiny. And you've learned that although you may not be able to control events, you can control the effects events have on you.

You are now aware that it isn't good enough to depend on chance, or on the whims of others, to build your future, and to make sure that you continue making progress on the road towards personal fulfillment. You are responsible for your own happiness or unhappiness. You also decided that you are the number one priority in your life, that improving your personality is more important than making improvements to your house, your wardrobe or your car.

The fuel of success

It isn't enough to decide to put your vehicle in gear if you want to move forward. You also need fuel to get you where you want to go.

Salespeople striving for success, managers, businesspeople, entrepreneurs, pharmacists, householders, electricians, parents - all of us need fuel. And this fuel, this combustible substance which keeps us going, is enthusiasm.

What is enthusiasm? Write down what you think it is:

Webster's dictionary says this word comes from enthous, entheos, which is the Greek for 'possessed by a god' (en, in, and theos, god). Therefore, enthusiasm gives us god-like power. Enthusiasm is like a fire, burning everything in its path and igniting the fuse of achievement. Enthusiasm is what drives us to create and to accomplish things, not education or even luck, although they can be helpful.

A great man once wrote: 'Nothing great is ever achieved without enthusiasm. With it, anything can be achieved. Enthusiasm can change the world.'

Focusing your entire being on attaining your goals

Enthusiasm is a force which focuses your entire being on attaining the goals you set for yourself. Once you have a goal, you throw yourself, body and mind, into whatever activities are required to achieve it, and you will succeed.

It is enthusiasm which has allowed all great people throughout history to accomplish what they did, both their own enthusiasm and the enthusiasm they generated in other people.

Take Rembrandt, for example. He dreamed about making a name for himself as a great painter, and was lucky enough to meet someone who became very enthusiastic about his early drawings and who encouraged him to continue.

Now, we may not be cut out to achieve greatness in the field of arts and letters, but we do all have something to accomplish here on earth. We all have a role to play. We are responsible for the society in which we live. We have something great to accomplish in our lifetime. Every person should be able to say, 'Humanity will have benefited because I exist'

Accomplishing great things

Perhaps you feel you're too young to do anything great? Well, what about Joan of Arc? She was only 19 when she led the French army to victory and liberated her country. Alexander the Great was 20 when he defeated the Asiatic hordes. Napoleon conquered Italy at the age of 25. Newton made most of his great discoveries before the age of 25. Victor Hugo wrote his first tragedy at 15 years of age.

Or perhaps you think you're too old? Well, de Gaulle was still the active leader of France when he was 76. Dandolo, the Doge of Venice, commanded an army at the age of 92! Doctor Johnson wrote his Life of the Poets when he was 78. Daniel Defoe wrote Robinson Crusoe when he was 85. James Watt learned to speak German when he was 85.

All these people were stimulated by their enthusiasm. The ideas that occurred to them provoked a series of actions; each of these actions led to a series of successes; each new success made them even more enthusiastic, and encouraged them to put their very best into achieving their goals.

Enthusiasm grows stronger in the face of obstacles

So what are you going to do? Enthusiasm has no age, gender or special conditions attached to it. Beware, however - there's a big difference between enthusiasm and nervous tension, which gets you all worked up about something, but then abandons you at the first sign of trouble.

Would you like to know if you're an enthusiastic person?

Think carefully about each of the following questions, and answer as honestly as you can.

[]   When someone proposes something new, do I get all excited about it?

[]   Do I give up easily when I encounter obstacles along the way?

[]   Am I capable of seeing something through to the end, even though everyone else doesn't agree with me?

[]   Have I ever been head of a parental, professional or political association?

[]   Am I interested in politics?

[]   Do my friends consider me an enthusiastic person?

[]   Do I consider myself young and vigorous?

[]   What do I hope to do in my old age?

[]   Am I able to animate a group of people by telling them a story or anecdote?

[]   Do I have a lot of friends?

[]   How many times a week do I usually go out with friends, or invite them over?

[]   Who is the most enthusiastic person I ever met in my life?

Now make a note of the areas where you feel you lack enthusiasm, and what you intend to do to improve the situation:

Epitaph: 'Dead at 25 – buried at 75'

Without enthusiasm, you grow old by the time you're 25. With it, age bas no meaning, and problems fall by the wayside. Being enthusiastic means having faith in life, faith in your abilities, faith in happiness and in humanity.

So how can you become enthusiastic? And how can you stay enthusiastic? Well, first you have to want it. You also have to resolve never to extinguish the flame of enthusiasm when you encounter it in others, and promise to develop your own enthusiasm, which can lead to great accomplishments and which makes anything possible.

You may have met a couple of 'extinguishers' yourself. How many people take pleasure, and even make it a duty, to try and extinguish other people's enthusiasm?

For example, a father might say to his son, 'My boy, stop dreaming! It's all very nice to want a career in --------------. But you should just accept the fact that you're not cut out for it.' Here the father is casting a kind of 'negative spell' on his son.

Or a woman might say to her husband, 'Just stay the way you are, you'll have a lot less problems that way.'

Think about all the negative suggestions we make to others without even realizing what we're doing.

What are the signs of enthusiasm?

What signs help you recognize enthusiasm in people? They have an air of assurance about them, a frank and open smile, and great curiosity; they are self-confident, sociable, idealistic and persevering. They are usually not overly shy, and never pessimistic.

Every one of us has a potential for greatness inside. Enthusiastic people transform this potential into reality by allowing their greatness to break through the boundaries of banality and mediocrity, all the petty problems of day-to-day existence.

Their enthusiasm shines through to the outside. We've already seen how we cannot act directly on our feelings. Instead we have to work on our body, on our exterior attitudes, in order to influence what is going on inside ourselves. So by training your body to adopt an enthusiastic attitude, you can influence your inner self.

With this aim in mind we're going to do an exercise, another 'mental sampling' designed to instill us with more enthusiasm. You are going to decide to be enthusiastic. Then, quite naturally, going to get your body to move in an enthusiastic way and you are to get it to adopt an enthusiastic attitude. The test will take care of itself.

Mental sampling:

I have decided to be enthusiastic and I act with enthusiasm.

Start your day by repeating this mental sampling: you'll say the words out loud, endowing your voice, your posture, your entire body with the attitude of an enthusiastic person. You'll soon see how enthusiasm will help you transform the world - first your inner world, and then the world around you.

An antidote to timidity and the lack of self confidence

When you're enthusiastic all your mental blocks, all the inhibitions which have been preventing you from fulfilling yourself, will fall by the wayside, one after the other.

Along with love, enthusiasm is the most positive emotion you can experience. You won't be able to think only about yourself any longer, carrying on with your self-centered ways. Instead you'll radiate person magnetism and concern yourself with the benefit of others.

How do you think great entertainers are able to mesmerize their audiences? How do you think great orators solicit such thunderous applause and admiration from their listeners.? It is simply because they are enthusiastic!

Now make a list of things you're enthusiastic about:

And what about this method? Are you enthusiastic about it too? Enthusiasm is also positive thinking: the ability to concentrate essentially on what is positive.

This week's schedule should include a few minutes

each day for talking to others about the benefits of this method. Just let people know what you are in the process of discovering: the inexhaustible wealth inside each and every one of us.

Summary

1.   Enthusiasm is a basic human need.

2.   Without enthusiasm, you are old at the age of 25.

3.   Enthusiasm has no age: it can be developed like physical strength, and can overcome all obstacles.

4.   Being enthusiastic means having faith in lire, in your abilities, in your happiness and in humanity.

5.   Enthusiastic people succeed in everything they do.

6.   Enthusiastic people are never bored and never feel isolated or abandoned. They attract others, and radiate energy and magnetism no matter how old they are.

7.   Enthusiasm transforms the world: first your inner world, and then the world around you. Enthusiasm is the antidote to timidity.

8.   Every one of us has a potential for greatness, but only enthusiasm can transform this potential into reality.

WEEK 7 -- SELF-EXPRESSION

This week we're going to think about self-expression, and work on improving the ways we express ourselves. Self-expression is the act of making what is hidden or contained inside you from outwards: in other words, exteriorizing.

Through self-expression you translate what you are carrying around inside, things other people and sometimes even you yourself are unaware of (for example, all the power and wealth of personality you didn't know you possessed) into comprehensible messages, so that you and others can understand them.

You are different

Self-expression means coming out of your shell and letting the best part of yourself shine out. That's right, I said the best of yourself. Obviously the juice of a plum tastes different from the juice of an orange or an apple. In the same way, the best of one person is not any better than the best of anyone else.

No two people are the same. I am different from anyone else, therefore I have to express myself in my own way, and not try to copy others. I have to respect others and accept the way they express themselves, which may not happen to be my way. This is very important, because no two people are exactly the same, and each and every one of us must express ourselves according to who we are.

So self-expression is like an act of creation. Everyone adds their own measure of originality. Being original doesn't necessarily mean being eccentric or strange. But it does mean being personal, expressing yourself in your own way, not repeating ready-made opinions or adopting other people's prejudices. Originality means manifesting your own personality in everything you do or say.

Expression is creation

There aren't many people who express themselves the way they should. Most only copy or imitate what others say to do, like an echo which reproduces sound, or a mirror which reflects a faithful image of whatever is placed in front of it. But true self expression is creation, not imitation or mimicry. You shouldn't model yourself after others, like a photographer who tries to reproduce a faithful image of someone else. Each person should express who they really are.

Have you ever been astonished to see yourself in a store window or in a mirror? 'What! Is that me? Do I really look that sad, that depressed, that tired?'

We express ourselves in many ways, one of them being the way we look. You don't have to talk to express who you are. Your face, your posture, your hands, your clothes are all expressions of your personality, of what you think and what you've experienced, your doubts and desires - in other words, who you are.

Do you think your education prepared you to express yourself properly? If only that were so! Unfortunately, most people grow up afraid to be different from others. It's almost as if we don't have the right to say what we think, to ask questions.

The key to happiness

Do you remember an incident in your life when you felt crushed by a teacher, a friend, a relative, or even by one of your parents, for one reason or another? Maybe you think you've forgotten all about it. But your subconscious has faithfully recorded the event, and without your knowing it this event is preventing you from expressing yourself as you are. If you were brought up by an authoritarian father, your subconscious remembers every detail. Today, although you are an adult, you may not act like one; you experience feelings of inferiority with other people. This feeling prevents you from expressing yourself the way you'd like, from bringing out the best of yourself. So you're not happy, because you cannot be happy if you can't express who you really are.

The basis of a successful education

Everyone should learn to exploit the best of themselves, according to their own original personality, and this process of education should begin in the cradle. If you had a negative education, try to avoid putting your children through the same thing.

How to communicate with the people around you

Of course, the most common way of expressing yourself is to communicate with the people around you. Ask yourself this question: what is the quality of the communication I have with my partner and my children?

There are moments when communication with out loved ones becomes more difficult, or more infrequent, and this is perfectly normal. Misunderstandings do arise from time to time. But you should never go to bed without at least trying to resolve a misunderstanding. Misunderstandings often arise because you decide to keep quiet instead of opening your heart and speaking frankly. And when you say something, try to express your impressions without attacking the other person! Instead of saying, 'Every time I tell a story you interrupt me and don't let me finish,' you can say something like: 'You know, whenever I tell a story I feel a certain pride in being able to express myself well. So when you interrupt me before I'm finished, I feel frustrated, and sometimes I get angry because I'm hurt.'

Learn to talk about your emotions:

- joy;
- sadness;
- anger;
- hurt;
- jealousy;
- pride;
- enthusiasm;
- anxiety;
- fear;
- love.

Try to find positive things to say to people. Compliment your partner and your children often. And when you have feelings, express them, especially when they're positive. Don't hide your feelings of love, joy, pride, admiration, esteem or respect.

Take stock of your communication skills

Would you like to know whether or not you express yourself the way you are? Think about each of the following questions carefully, and answer as honestly as you can:

- Am I a closed person, someone who shuts off from others easily?
- Do I feel hurt by the slightest criticism?
- Am I often considered the life of a party?
- Is it easy for me to express my feelings of anger, hurt, respect, love and joy?
- Has my partner ever reproached me for not communicating enough?
- Do I prefer remaining silent rather than stating my opinions about things?
- Do I like to sing and make people laugh when I'm at a party?
- Do I enjoy speaking in public?
- Am I a shy person who gets uncomfortable easily?
- Do I play an active role in groups, associations,

political movements?

- Do I express myself through painting, poetry, music, literature or some other form of artistic endeavor?
- Who is the person I admire the most? Why?
- What kind of books do I like reading best? Who are my favorite authors? What do they mean to me?
- Do I have a hard time asking people for help?
- Are (or were) my mother and father able to express their feelings easily?
- What are my ambitions?

Are there any specific subjects, any areas where you tend to have trouble expressing yourself? What can you do to remedy this? Is there something you always dreamed of doing one day? What is it? How can you make this dream a reality? Make a note of your thoughts:

Body language

Your body is a marvelous means of expression. You can and should use your entire body to express yourself. How?

Everything about us says something: the way we look at people, the way we walk, out gestures, our clothes, our posture.

Take up a new activity

We express ourselves with our hands, in paintings, drawings, using brushes and hammers, pencils, the earth itself, flowers, wood, iron, glass or paper. We express ourselves through singing, dance, sporting activities, through knitting and music, ceramics.., the list is endless.

And, you know, it's never too late to start. Why not have a go at it? In our 'society of leisure' no one can be entirely fulfilled without learning some means of self-expression, using the varied and marvelous instruments of expression the modem world has placed at our disposition.

Why not tape your own voice, listen to it and try to improve it? All you need is a tape recorder. Take a cooking course, a computer course, learn a new language, take singing lessons, dancing, or learn salsa. Knitting can be fun. You can commit yourself to improving your vocabulary, by looking up new words that you hear or read in the dictionary every day, making sure you understand exactly what they mean; or learn a new language, through classes and on holiday, make your own web page, take singing lessons.

This will make your life a hundred times more enjoyable, and will have a positive effect on the people around you as well. A whole world will open up for you as soon as you decide you really want to express yourself. What is the point of knowing people if you can't express yourself to them'? Unfortunately, many people express only a tiny amount of what is inside them and what they are capable of doing. How about you'?

Become a 'master' of self-expression

You have to start with yourself. You have to open up, get rid of the mask you're hiding behind. You have to be able to sing, laugh, converse or smile, without caring what others might think about you, without any false pride, without being afraid of making a fool of yourself. You have to be able to dance with children, sing and laugh with them, tell them stories that spring from your imagination. If you can play with children you can do anything you want.

You also have to learn to be 'exciting'. We admire actors, singers, speakers or writers who excite us, because they themselves are exciting. You have to learn to be exciting, to admire the world around you and exclaim your admiration to one and all; you have to be passionate about something. And this can be learned, just as you can learn to dance or play the piano.

Awaken the great person sleeping inside you

All great historical figures are like that: they get excited about something, and then they act. And there's a great person lying dormant inside each and every one of us, inside me and inside you: all you have to do is wake them up.

One day Pope Julius II saw Michelangelo hammering away at a block of marble, all covered in dust, and asked, 'But why are you hammering so hard, my dear man?' Michelangelo replied, 'Don't you see the angel imprisoned in the block of stone? I have to get it out.'

That should give you some food for thought. There is an imprisoned angel in all of us, a great human being whom we are ignoring. We must work to free this imprisoned angel, and exploit the untold riches we possess, for the benefit of those around us.

The block of marble is like the mask we wear, rigid with prejudices and the fear of showing ourselves as we really are.

A great humanist once wrote: 'Human beings make use of barely 10 to 20 per cent of their capacities.' There's no time to waste. We must start today to concentrate out energies on expressing the best of ourselves. We can do it.

But be careful! You can't keep a bow stretched to the limit all day long, and neither should you remain excited for too long at a time. You also have to relax, and mobilize your energy for tomorrow's tasks. We live in a stressful world, full of tension, frayed nerves, worry and anxiety. We often sleep without being really relaxed, and we wake up the next morning still tired from the day before. It takes luck to find a caring, compassionate boss. People too often resort to pills, alcohol and other stimulants to cope, looking for artificial ways to relax. Even holidays don't help if we do not know how to relax.

Relax and work better

The first thing you have to learn is to take the time to relax. You don't have any choice in the matter. Have you ever noticed that it's often the busiest people who find the time to read? That's because they make the time.

Everything around us creates tension: noise, bright lights, late nights, children, tight schedules. We don't have time for ourselves, time to just live, rest, read and relax. We don't seem to have time to do anything for ourselves any more, and don't know how to cope.

The answer lies in learning to relax. You can accomplish a lot more work when you're relaxed than when you're tense. Someone who has so much housework to do they don't know where to begin gets stressed and impatient, and does the work much less effectively. They have to learn to relax. A doctor who thinks she has to do everything herself because she doesn't know how to relax will also become overwrought and less effective. She too must learn to relax.

And by relaxing I don't mean lounging around, I mean using your mind to relax all your muscles. When your body is completely relaxed you cannot feel any negative emotions. We're negative when we're nervous, and experience only positive feelings when we are relaxed.

Once you decide to express yourself better, to exploit the best of yourself, you may find you get a little discouraged from time to time because of the obstacles you are likely to encounter. Well, don't give up. And remember that relaxation is the cornerstone of your success. Everything else, and I mean everything, will fall right into place.

I hope you understand a little better just how important relaxation is for reaching your goal. It is crucial. You'll soon be reading a whole chapter on the subject of relaxation.

This week I want you to concentrate on overcoming your fears about expressing who you really are, about being exciting, about admiring the world around you, and expressing yourself in your own personal and original way.

Summary

1. Expressing yourself means bringing out the very best of yourself.
2. The best part of you is not necessarily the best part of someone else.
3. We all have to express ourselves the way we are.
4. Your entire being is a means of expression.
5. You will never be happy unless you are able to express who you are.
6. In order to express yourself fully, you have to know how to relax.

WEEK 8 -- SUGGESTION

I'm sure you've had a marvelous week, taking full advantage of your newfound ability to express the real you. Perhaps you even discovered things about yourself you didn't know were there, hidden talents just waiting for an opportunity to shine through.

This was just the beginning. Once you master the techniques of suggestion and complete relaxation, you will see some profound changes taking place in your lire. These two things - suggestion and relaxation - are closely linked. You cannot fully exploit the benefits of suggestion unless you are able to relax completely. And you can't relax completely without making use of the power of suggestion. In this chapter we'll be talking mainly about suggestion. Relaxation is covered in the next chapter.

Using the power of Suggestion to your advantage

Suggestion is an extremely important technique which can change our lives if we know how to use it to our advantage and fully exploit its potential, but it is very often misunderstood. In this chapter I'm going to give you some idea of the benefits of the power of suggestion, and help you apply it in your daily life.

Everyone wants to be happy, healthy and successful. However, as I'm sure you've noticed, what life has in store for us isn't always what we want, and we often have to deal with sickness, failure and unhappiness. Why does this happen? Well, the underlying reason is that we don't always strive to obtain what we want.

On a conscious level you, like me, want only good things to happen; however, what does your subconscious want? Remember, whatever happens to you has been prepared by your subconscious, because you have commanded it to do so.

Let's try to see a little more clearly how this works. What is the subconscious? What is suggestion?

What is suggestion?

A suggestion is an idea which influences us without

our knowing. You know how children stop feeling pain when Mummy 'kisses it better'. You may have heard about dentists who are able to use the power of suggestion as an anesthetic, painlessly extracting teeth without resorting to drugs. Or hypnotists who can help people stop smoking. These people have learned how to make use of the extraordinary power of suggestion, and have found various applications for it in their professional lives. Why not do the same, and apply this amazing technique in your own life?

Here's how it works: your conscious mind can influence your subconscious in exactly the same way that a hypnotist can. The more confident we are, the more effective our suggestions will be. So by making positive suggestions, you attract health, success and happiness.

The relationship between our conscious and subconscious minds is a little like that of a boss and a secretary. The boss runs the office, while the secretary carries out the boss's orders to the letter.

Now suppose that the boss and secretary don't know each other very well and have trouble understanding each other. Suppose the boss isn't doing a very good job running the office. The secretary, although trying to do everything possible to assure that things run smoothly, may occasionally do things which annoy the boss, postponing payment to a supplier which the boss wanted to send immediately, for example, or sending a letter the boss didn't want to send just yet.

Our subconscious: the perfect executor

Our subconscious is a little like the secretary in the above analogy. But the secretary in out mind never forgets anything, records absolutely everything that happens, and executes our deepest wishes, even if what we want is harmful to our well-being. The subconscious simply executes what it is ordered to do, like a computer. It is a perfect executor, and does everything it is told to do.

A simple example may help you understand. Suppose you're having trouble remembering someone's name. 'You know ... he used to come here almost every day ... it's on the tip of my tongue

This is where the boss - your conscious mind - comes in. You give your subconscious an order to remember this name. Then you go and do something else. All the while your subconscious is running through its files, searching for the name, just like a computer, without your even realizing it. And suddenly, when you're least expecting it, the name pops into your head.

We've all had the following experience: we're trying to recall a name, and the more we try the more impossible it becomes. Like the boss in the above example, it's useless to go hunting through files when there's a secretary who can do the job much better, and without getting tired.

But now suppose you say to yourself, 'I'm losing my memory! I must be getting old,' after which you forget about it. Had you known about the consequences, you wouldn't have allowed yourself to think that. Why? Because without knowing it you send a command to your subconscious, which immediately gets to work on creating a loss of memory, exactly as you are ordering it to do. Your subconscious does whatever you command it to do, without judging whether the command is positive or negative. So you can understand just how important positive mental orientation is.

Your subconscious is like a mechanical secretary, executing commands without ever getting tired. It is essential that you train it to work for you instead of against you, that you have confidence in its abilities and delegate certain tasks to it instead of trying to do everything yourself, as many bosses tend to do. If you learn to make full use of your subconscious you will be absolutely amazed at what it can do for you, multiplying your present capacities a hundredfold and helping you realize your most ambitious projects.

Be careful about the kinds of 'mental commands' you send your

subconscious

We very often order our subconscious to do things we don't really want to do. But it faithfully goes about its work, without discriminating, simply 'following orders'. For example, every spring I might say something like, 'All right, it's spring again, and I'll probably catch the flu.' Without knowing it I have just sent a command to my subconscious. Or you might say something like, 'Oh no, it's ironing day, I can feel my headache coming on already.' And your subconscious sets to work, creating the conditions favorable for catching the flu or getting a headache. 'Your headache is ready! And your flu is on the way!'

Your subconscious can make you healthy if you send it the right commands. It can also make you sick, tired and unlikely to succeed if you send it those kinds of commands. Your subconscious does not discriminate, it doesn't sort and separate negative commands from positive ones. It simply executes your commands as faithfully as it can.

People don't die, they kill themselves

Human beings are capable of exploring the depths of the oceans and the universe, but often ignore the depths of their own minds. A great French scientist wrote, 'Man is the unknown. People don't die, they kill themselves.'

Don't you find it amazing that there is an incredible computer inside you, capable of executing your slightest command? It is, however, up to you to assume control, to provide it with constructive commands which led to your happiness and success. And all these commands, these orders, are what we call 'suggestions'.

The power of suggestion is vast. It can heal us, or it can hurt us. But it cannot perform miracles.

When you start using the power of suggestion many of the obstacles which, up to now, have barred your path will become springboards on the road to a better life. You'll overcome all such obstacles with ease, as soon as you acquire an unshakable confidence in your strength and your abilities. And how can you acquire such confidence? By mastering the technique of suggestion and relaxation.

You won't recognize yourself

Of course, we can only provide you with the basics of suggestion training. Your continuing study and constant practice of personal development will help develop your understanding of the subject, as you experience its effects and learn more about its history, its nature, the various categories of suggestion, and the conditions which make it most effective. In time you will master the technique and use it to transform your life, to the point where you won't recognize yourself any longer.

At the same time your children, friends, students, colleagues, partner - all the people you associate with - will benefit. Because suggestion lies at the heart of our relationships with others. Educating children is, in fact, nothing more than making a series of suggestions, and re-educating ourselves is entirely based on the technique of suggestion.

So it's important to learn to get along with your subconscious, and exploit its riches. It's important to know how to make use of it when educating out' children. Because we are all the sure of the suggestion made to us when we were children. Many illnesses, behavior and aptitude problems often attributed to our genetic make-up are often nothing more than the results of negative suggestions.

What 'evil spells' were cast on you in the form of negative suggestions ?

Do you remember, when you were a child, hearing things like:

- I'm not surprised, you're always late.
- Don't cry like that, you're not a little child!
- You never listen to what I say!
- Just like a man!

- Life is hard!
- You're so lazy!
- Being called names like 'fatty', 'sacredly cat' or 'stupid'.

If only we could have recognized such statements for what they really are - criminal attacks which can mark a child for life, negative suggestions that can actually turn a child into a lazy or fearful or timid adult. Because all these negative suggestions, these judgments and prejudices, remain recorded in our subconscious mind. They are veritable 'evil spells' cast by the people around us. And unless we break them, they can affect us for our entire lives.

Give your subconscious a chance to work in peace

Let's get back to our initial comparison of a boss and secretary: our mental boss provides our secretary with a general directive and a broad outline of how to proceed, as well as a deadline, saying, 'I need this done for such and such a day, at such and such a time.' But then what happens? The boss keeps walking into the secretary's office and asking, 'Well, how's it going? Are you making progress? Are you sure it'll be finished on time? Do you think you can handle it?'

This only exasperates the secretary and makes the

work that much harder. What should happen is that, after giving an order, the boss should let the secretary get on with the work in peace.

In the same way, it's very important not to get nervous or worried after giving your subconscious an order. Instead, you should let it do its work in peace. And to create the best possible conditions for the subconscious to function effectively, you have to know how to practice relaxation. You must start with relaxation if you want to master the technique of suggestion fully.

That's why, since the start of this method, I suggested you do some daily relaxation exercises. Only when we're in a state of relaxation can our subconscious work effectively to create the conditions favorable for our success and happiness. If you are tense, nervous or worried, your subconscious will only create more problems, just like the child who starts screaming because everyone else in the room is tense and nervous.

Praise your subconscious and it will serve you better

Suppose the boss notices that the secretary always carries out orders, whether they make good sense or not. The boss then says, 'Well, I'd better make sure all my orders make good sense.'

And in fact it is up to you to order your subconscious to do things that will make you happy.

Suppose, on the other hand, that a buss is continually reprimanding the secretary, never offering a word of encouragement, only picking out faults. Don't you think their relationship might get a little tense?

Well, that's exactly what happens with our subconscious: too often a struggle for domination develops, and this results in enormous tension. We create tension when we reprimand out subconscious by thinking things like:

- Well, that's me all over again! How could I be so stupid!
- I knew this would happen, I just knew it.
- I'm such an idiot!
- I can't stand myself!
- If there's some way to screw up, you can be sure I'll find it!
- That's typical of the way I am.

Make a list of the ways you think about yourself. If necessary ask people you know if they can remember your exact words?

How many of these negative thoughts could you have avoided, if you'd only known what devastating effects they have, not to mention all the negative suggestions made by others (the 'criminal suggestions' I mentioned earlier)?

Your subconscious 'files'

Every one of these negative suggestions is recorded and stored in your subconscious files, just like the files in a secretary's office. Our subconscious works in more or less the same way.

Say, for example, I have to meet someone. My subconscious immediately gets to work retrieving files with information about all my previous meetings with people, right back to when I was an infant. It classifies all the files and adds them up: 1,382 files marked Meetings; out of that total there may be 1,278 files marked Unsatisfactory Meetings, and 104 marked Positive Meetings.

Based on this data my subconscious will do everything it can to dissuade me from attending the meeting. I'll start to feel jittery, my palms will start sweating, I may tremble and blush. I'll forget the name of the person I'm supposed to meet, I'll get all tongue-tied, and so on. In the end I'll say, 'I knew it! I shouldn't have gone.'

The same kind of thing happens in countless other situations: in our relations with the opposite sex, educating our children, giving birth, writing exams, dealing with our fears, phobias, and so on.

Do this experiment

Take a moment to look into one of your subconscious files. For example, try to relive in your mind an event which happened to you in the past, and from which you feel you learned something. Then ask yourself if what you learned was positive or negative.

For example, say you relive your first date, and find you felt completely ridiculous and vowed never to go out on a date again! Well, you can assume that the lesson you learned was not very positive.

Take a few minutes to write down your experiences, and what you learned from them:

Do you get along with your subconscious?

What is the most negative thing someone has told me, which I feel has harmed me the most?

What is the most positive thing someone has told me, which I feel has helped me the most?

[] Do I ever think things like 'I can't do it, I'll never be able to do it, I'm too old to change'?

[] Do I quickly become impatient when something I undertake doesn't go my way?

[] Do I ever say things like 'I'm not good enough!'

or 'I'm so stupid!'?

[]   Am I in the habit of blaming myself for things I do badly?

[]   Do I ever congratulate myself when I succeed?

[]   Do I ever feel sad without knowing why?

[]   Am I obsessed about anything?

[]   Are most of the thoughts that pop into my mind optimistic or pessimistic ?

[]   Do I have faith in my abilities? Do I have confidence in events, other people and in myself?

[]   Do I ever talk badly about myself, belittle myself in front of others?

[]   Do I have a good memory for names, events, numbers places, dates, details, times, languages?

What areas of my life would I like to improve through suggestion: health, work, productivity, personality?

What hidden riches have I discovered in mysel. since beginning this method?

Don't you think it's about time your conscious and subconscious minds got together and did some real housecleaning of your subconscious files? From now on, you must set aside all negative suggestions. The files you're going to keep from now on will contain only positive messages.

You'll need to give yourself a little time. You can't

become an entirely positive person in just a few weeks, after spending 20, 30, 40 or more years with a tendency to orient your mind in negative ways. So first of all, start by relaxing. Because if you get impatient you'll get tense, and as we've already explained, when you're tense your subconscious works against you, just like a secretary who makes mistakes because the boss is on their back all the time.

Congratulate yourself

You also know that it's important for a boss to congratulate a secretary from time to time. Occasional praise is actually indispensable, if relations between them are to be harmonious. The same applies to your subconscious. You outline what you want it to do, place your confidence in it, and then let it work in peace.

And when it fulfils your request, you must congratulate yourself. If your subconscious makes a mistake, you forgive yourself, just as a boss forgives a secretary for an error. This is all the more important when you remember that we ourselves are responsible for the errors committed by our subconscious. Either we disturbed it and didn't allow it to get on with its work, or we were not confident enough in its abilities.

Do you understand now why self-confidence is the foundation of a happy, fulfilling life?

To summarize, your conscious and subconscious minds must learn to live in harmony with each other if you want to achieve what is right and good for you. To accomplish this, your conscious mind sets the outlines of a plan, and your subconscious takes care of the details. Your conscious mind lets your subconscious work in peace, congratulating it when it succeeds, never being aggressive when it fails, but rather excusing it and encouraging it to do better the next time, showing where it went wrong and suggesting a better alternative. You must 'tame' your subconscious mind, educate it as you would a child, or the way you'd train a dog. You have to have confidence in it, and hot be afraid to ask too much of it - since it never gets tired - while at the same time being patient and not expecting instant results.

How to formulate your suggestions

You must always formulate your suggestions in a positive way when communicating with your subconscious. For example, don't say, 'I am not impatient.' First of all this isn't true, and second it constitutes a negative suggestion. Don't say things like 'I am not tired, I am not shy, I am not angry.' Instead, use words like 'more', 'more and more' and 'already'. Say things like 'I already feel more relaxed' or 'I already feel calmer' or 'I feel more and more self-confident' or 'I'm feeling better and better', and so on.

Now here is an exercise in suggestion which you should do every day, after your breathing and relaxation exercises.

Repeat this formulation ten times, breathing deeply:

Every day

in all ways

I feel better and better.

Of course, this is a very general suggestion: in time you'll gradually start making more practical, more specific suggestions.

You will find a complete suggestion session at the end of this chapter. And don't forget to create your own formulations, tailored to suit your specific needs. Think carefully before you use them, making sure they are simple and easy to understand, and above all that they are positive.

Keep planting your suggestions in your subconscious mind until they become firmly anchored, until they are an integral part of your life and are transformed into action in the form of positive habits.

Through suggestion you can learn to sleep better, be more relaxed, become a better educator for your children, a better salesperson or a more caring partner. You will take pleasure in discovering the amazing power of this instrument of success, this marvelous companion called the subconscious mind.

To get the most out of your suggestion sessions, don't forget to relax first. Only when your body is completely relaxed does your subconscious become completely receptive: and that is the moment you should make your suggestions. Do this in the morning after waking up, in the evening before going to sleep, and whenever you feet the need during the day.

Complete general suggestion session

Get comfortable in a quiet location, in a position you find relaxing. Make sure there isn't too much light so you won't be distracted. After ten deep breaths, you can start the general suggestion exercise. For the first few weeks do the exercise every day, at the same time and under the same conditions whenever possible. Read the text out loud slowly, in a clear voice, or tape it, making sure to adopt a positive and self-assured tone. This is very important.

First, I understand that everything I say will remain firmly engraved on my mind. The words I hear will remain imprinted on my mind for ever, without my wanting or even knowing it, completely subconsciously. My mind and my entire being will absorb what I say and obey my commands.

The first thing I tell myself is that every day, three times a day, in the morning, at noon and in the evening, in other words at mealtimes, I will be hungry. I will experience a pleasant sensation of hunger which will make me look forward to eating with pleasure. And I will take pleasure in eating, without overeating. I'll take care to chew my food well, transforming it into a kind of soft paste which can be swallowed easily. This will help me digest well, so that I feel no heaviness or discomfort in my stomach or intestines, no pain of any kind.

My body will assimilate the foods I eat properly, and use them to produce blood, muscles, new cells, strength and energy - in other words, to promote life.

Also, every night, from as soon as I want to go to sleep until the moment I want to wake up next morning, I will enter into a deep, calm, regenerating sleep, so that when I wake up I'll feel refreshed and enthusiastic about the day ahead.

Although I sometimes got sad or depressed in the past, I do not any longer. From now on, instead of being sad or depressed, instead of sulking and brooding, I feel I'll be a joyous, optimistic person, for no special reason but just because that's how I am. And even if I have real cause to worry, I'll understand that worrying won't accomplish anything and I'll remain optimistic.

If, in the past, I sometimes got angry or impatient, I won't allow these emotions to get the better of me any longer. On the contrary, I'll be patient, always in control of myself, completely unaffected by the things that used to bother or irritate me. I am calm, very calm. Instead of taking what happens personally, I'll be more objective, I'll see other people's points of view, and solutions to my problems will appear easily, almost magically.

If I am sometimes haunted by negative thoughts that are both harmful and unhealthy for me, fears, temptations, resentment and so on, I understand that these will enter my mind more and more rarely, and will soon disappear completely, just as a dream dissolves when you wake up in the morning.

Another very important point is that if I felt a certain lack of self-confidence in the past, I will now feel more and more confident, based in the incalculable strength I have discovered in myself. I know that this confidence is absolutely necessary for every human being.

With self-confidence I can accomplish anything I choose, within reason. My self-confidence is growing day by day, and this confidence fills me with the certainty that I am capable of accomplishing anything I want, as long as it is within reason and of benefit to others and to myself.

So when I want something or want to accomplish something, I will always know that my desire is attainable. And I will attain it, quickly, without getting fatigued, without effort.

It will be easy for me to see things through to the end, to make my projects a success. I am able to express my feelings and thoughts more and more easily every day, and I am liberating the infinite potential which is in me.

Now I am going to come out of my state of relaxation. And when I do I will feel completely rested, full of vigor, alert, ready for action, full of energy and lire. I will also be positive, joyous, optimistic and open in all my relations with people, and in everything I do.

I am going to repeat this very simple, very effective formulation ten to twenty times every day, morning and evening:

> **Every day**
> **in all ways**
> **I feel better and better.**

(Adapted from Emile Coué's famous formulation)

Summary

1. Suggestions do not merely stuff your brain with useless ideas, they are 'commands you make to yourself'.

2. Suggestions communicate what your conscious mind wants your subconscious mind to do, so that it can work for you.

3. Suggestions are ideas which are carried out without our knowing.

4. The subconscious mind is a perfect executor, faithfully carrying out whatever it is ordered to do. It never gets tired, and never forgets.

5. Your conscious mind can influence your subconscious mind in the same way that a hypnotist can influence a subject.

6. Therefore, the more confident and aware your conscious mind is, the more effective your suggestions will be.

7. By learning to get your subconscious to work for you, you multiply your capacities. By using the technique of positive suggestion, you can make your subconscious work for your happiness and success.

8. It takes a little time to learn how to make your subconscious work for you.

9. The techniques of suggestion and relaxation form the basis of your new life.

10. You are worth a hundred times more than you think.

WEEK 9 -- RELAXATION

Now let's talk about relaxation.

Relaxation has been mentioned numerous times in previous chapters, but it is so important that we are going to devote an entire chapter to it here. Relaxation can be a problem for many people. Either they think they don't have the time, or they don't know what techniques to use.

And as we said, relaxation and suggestion are very closely linked: you can't master one without the other. You have already started taking advantage of the power of suggestion, but you cannot take full advantage of it if you don't learn how to relax completely.

Fortunately, it is something which can be learned - and it's well worth the effort. Knowing how to relax can transform your life.

You know that you can exercise direct control over your body. And you also know that if you want to influence your mind or your emotions, you have to work through the body, through your muscles, posture, breathing, taking cold or lukewarm showers, and so on. You know that by changing your exterior attitude, you can also change your state of mind. And since you can change your exterior attitude - in other words your body - at will, you are in a sense 'immunized' against negative sensations like anger, impatience, boredom, depression, and so on. All you have to do is observe your exterior attitude and make changes whenever necessary. Changing the expression on your face changes your state of mind.

Changing your mental scenery

You can use suggestion to create mental images of happiness, calm, joy - images of relaxation. You can change your mental scenery at will, rather as you change the slide in a projector: just click forward and the image changes from a storm to one of serene sunshine. You can do exactly the same thing in your mind by controlling your breathing. Take a single series of deep breaths and you can transform a gray and dismal mental image into one of light and calm, serenity, peace, joy, love of life ... in other words, relaxation.

So from now on, whenever you feel tired or annoyed,

depressed or exhausted, don't resort to stimulants or tranquillizers for a solution. Create new positive mental images to replace those that are dark and despairing, and run them across the screen of your mind - images of calm, relaxed serenity and joy. If you find this difficult, try to work on your body, doing things that bring up positive images: breathe deeply, get loose and comfortable, the rest will come. Your tension will disappear.

No action without tension

Some measure of tension is necessary for any kind of activity. We have to channel our energy towards the goal we have in mind. Without tension we wouldn't accomplish anything in life. But there's good tension and bad tension. The kind we have to eliminate, the bad kind, is the tension that arises before and/or after the effort required to accomplish the task at hand.

For example, I have to generate some tension, I have to 'get energized' to make a sale, teach a course or do my writing. But if, when I finish working, I keep mulling over what I should or could have done, then I become needlessly tense: I waste my energy instead of using it. I'm also wasting energy when I spend half of today planning what I'm going to do tomorrow. What I should be doing is relaxing, mobilizing my energy for the moment when I really need it.

Unfortunately, most people are only partially relaxed when they work, and remain partially tense when they relax. They cannot concentrate as fully as they should on their work, which results in poor productivity. When they try to relax they cannot forget about their work, and only achieve a half measure of real relaxation. This situation leads to burn-out, depression and anxiety.

Life's three phases

Life is a series of repeated phases: the active phase, when body and mind are in movement; rest, during which faculties and muscles are on standby; and finally sleep, where bodily functions slow down and the conscious mind does not operate.

These three states of consciousness are essential for maintaining life and renewing the energy we spend. But people too often ignore the basic principles which regulate these three phases. Instead, they get trapped in an infernal circle where their active lives become agitated, their rest periods are usually not restful since they car hardly find the time to relax, and even sleep, which should restore their energies, escapes them so that they awaken fatigued, sluggish and depressed.

Their muscles are often not fully relaxed even in phases of rest or sleep, and neuromuscular tension prevents the body from recuperating rapidly. Cerebral mechanisms keep on functioning, often intensely, seemingly out of control, giving rise to obsessions, nightmares and other forms of anxiety.

Acquiring a new outlook

Therefore, mastering the art of relaxation is extremely important. But relaxation is not just a momentary muscular release, nor is it limited to a few exercises. Real relaxation, the result of mental and physical balance, is a whole new way of life, a series of positive habits which you must acquire in order to replace your old negative ones.

You aren't going to find any formulas for relaxation here. Instead, we're going to think about a few simple things which will lead you to the path of true relaxation.

Causes of nervous tension

There are a number of factors which can create nervous tension: latent worries about your future, political events which create a climate of uncertainty, unsatisfactory working conditions, social grievances, ideological struggles, economic problems ... all these tend to put your future in doubt, and thus create nervous tension.

On a personal level, our senses are also subject to stress. We are constantly being exposed to a barrage of sensory stimulations such as ambient noise, city traffic, flashing TV images, and so on, which give out nervous system no respite, creating a climate of stress which becomes like a drug we think we can't do without. This kind of permanent 'white noise' wears down the nervous system over time.

We also have all our professional, family and personal problems to deal with. A host of minor obstacles seem to be constantly hovering around our lives, resulting in a variety of circumstances which create tension in body and mind, or in a specific part of the body.

Types of tension also vary: minor and intense, physical and mental, temporary and permanent, superficial or profound. Tension can be encountered anywhere: on a street corner, at the office, in the workshop, within relationships, or at home with your family. There is also a distinction between conscious and unconscious tension. You may be consciously irritated by noise from the street, or you may not even notice it. Nevertheless, your nervous system suffers the consequences. You may become tense because you are consciously worrying about something, but you can also be stressed because of an unconscious complex or psychological 'block' which shows up in your body in the form of involuntary tension.

Measure your ability to relax

Would you like to know if you are able to relax? Think about each of the following questions carefully, and answer as truthfully as you can:

[] Have I ever taken a course or used some kind of method to help me relax (sophrology, alpha relaxation, yoga, meditations, some form of physical exercise)?

[] Am I in good health?

[] Do I digest my food well? Do I sleep well?

[] Do I feel nervous? Anxious? Overworked?

[] Do I have any nervous habits: wetting my lips, biting my nails, uncontrolled giggling, playing with my hair, coughing, doodling?

[] Do I have trouble keeping still? Do I do things like drum my fingers on the table, tap my foot, jiggle my leg?

[] Do I smoke?

[] Do I use alcohol as a pick-me-up?

[] Do I take pills to help me sleep, stimulate my appetite, help with my digestion, calm me down?

[] Do I often find myself worrying about fears that never materialize?

[] Are the people I live with anxious? Were my mother and/or father anxious?

[] How many hours a day do I have the TV or

radio turned on?

[]   Do I lose my temper easily?

[]   Do I jump at the slightest noise?

[]   Has anyone ever told me I was nervous or tense?

[]   Do I often feel my nerves are on edge?

[]   Are my children and/or my partner nervous?

[]   Am I interested in relaxation?

Live in a permanent state of relaxation

Am I generally tense? What is causing this tension inside me? Where does it come from? How is it expressed? Are there any exterior causes? Are these the real causes, or are they only apparent? If not, what are the real causes? What can I do to counteract this? How can I relax my tensed-up muscles ? Well, what you should be aiming for is a state of permanent relaxation, but you can only attain that through patient, daily relaxation sessions.

These questions are important because the battle is already half won as soon as you know where your tension is coming from. Then all you have to do is want to overcome it, and do everything necessary to accomplish this.

Indicate here where you think your tension comes from, and the ways in which you show or express it:

What is the nervous system?

Do you remember what we said about the wholeness of human beings? People are composed of two parts, body and mind, which although distinct are closely united. This unity is maintained through the brain and the nervous system. The brain creates the link between the physical and mental. One part of the brain is responsible for generating and storing thoughts and emotions. Now where does the nervous system enter into all this? What is it, exactly?

I'm not about to offer you a course in physiology, but it is important to know a little about your nervous system if you want it to function normally. Let's just say that the nervous system is like a large telephone switchboard which receives and transmits messages to our entire being. These messages come from out external senses -vision, hearing, touch - and from out internal senses - imagination, memory, and so on.

All our thoughts, images and ideas are based on these sensory messages. They are continually being sent to the brain, which then responds to them. For example, if you place your hand on a hot iron, your sense of touch will send a message to your brain. Finding the heat a bit intense, your brain will respond by sending another message, ordering your muscles to remove your hand. Of course, all this happens in a fraction of a second. But what you should remember is that every time your brain receives a message, its response affects your entire body.

This is what happens, for example, when I get a phone call announcing a friend's visit. I send the message to my brain, which then responds through my body: I smile, hum, I feel happy. But if the taxman calls and announces he's going to spend two months going through my books, I will react quite differently: I'll worry, brood, sleep badly.

Your brain is continually receiving and sending messages, often without your knowing. You're not always aware that surrounding noises, lights, smells, sounds and other stimuli are being perceived, transmitted and responded to by your brain. Nevertheless, they are.

Overloading the nervous system: doing the same work 3 times

It's not unusual for the nervous system to become overloaded. You know you shouldn't overload an electrical circuit, so you don't plug your iron, toaster, microwave, hair dryer and fridge into the same socket all at the same time.

Some people overload their nervous system all the time. Result? They always feel on edge, highly stressed, overworked. They invariably end up exploding, because they haven't learned to disconnect before they connect. Once your work is done you have to disconnect yourself from it, in other words forget about it, and plug into something else.

But too many people forget to disconnect themselves, and end up doing the same work three times: once while preparing to do it, once while actually doing it, and a third time when they've finished, by torturing themselves with thoughts of what they could or should have done differently. They never manage to relax, because they're always plugged in.

You have to learn to disconnect everything, your entire being. If you live under the constant pressure of intense emotions, you become overloaded and risk exploding. So it's very important not to keep your organism 'plugged in' all day long, all your life. You have to learn to disconnect yourself, especially in the context of modern urban life, which places relentless stress on all our senses and all our nerves.

A few examples of sensory overload

Our vision is being constantly disturbed by lights that are too bright, by flashy neon signs, exposure to the sun, TV and computer screens, and so on.

Out sense of taste is severely stressed by all the non-natural or harmful substances we ingest - alcohol, cigarettes, caffeine.

Our hearing is constantly attacked by ambient noise, shouting, household appliances, music, other people's walkmans, videos, advertising, screeching tires, noises from building sites. Some people have become so used to noise they actually become anxious when their surroundings are silent!

Our sense of smell suffers from all the pollution encountered in cities, the smell of petrol and exhaust fumes, factory emissions, badly ventilated living and working areas, and so on.

As for out sense of touch, it too is affected by the tight clothing we wear, by our sedentary lifestyles, even by our own minds, as we tend to become more and more introverted, concerned only with our own thoughts, so that we almost forget how to touch.

Then there's the effect of various media on out minds and sensitivity: horror films, daily reports of violence, crime, wars, assassinations, catastrophes, and so on.

The world we live in is overloaded with stress, bursting at the seams with tension. And the worst thing is that most people don't even realize it!

Indicate what you find stressful about your own surroundings:

So you have to take care of your nervous system. If you have any doubts about whether or not your nervous system is balanced and functioning properly, consult a specialist.

But let's assume that your nervous system is in good shape, organically speaking. In that case you have to take steps to keep it functioning properly.

3/4 of disorders are functional

I just used two words: 'organic' and 'functional'. An organic illness means that an organ is physically damaged. If I get a bullet in the lungs, the organ is organically affected. If I contract cancer of the intestine, my intestines become organically ill.

In functional illnesses the organ itself is healthy, although you feel that 'something is not quite right'. Too often doctors will tell you there's nothing wrong with you, which means that the tests they conduct, the X-rays and blood analysis and so on, have shown nothing abnormal. It means that you are suffering from an illness that is not organic, but functional.

Almost 75 per cent of all reported illnesses have some functional element, and can become organic. If you allow yourself to remain in a state of anxiety for too long you may very well develop an ulcer, for example.

Functional disorders mostly arise from negative ways of thinking and behaving. Our distorted thought patterns are the underlying causes of most of out health problems. We don't know how to manage our nervous system properly, ignoring conditions necessary for mental and physical hygiene, so that we don't give our nervous system a chance to function properly.

Suggestion can help you remedy this situation. But once again, you must learn to manage your nervous system and treat it properly so that the suggestions you make can take effect. You have to make sure to provide your nervous system with everything it needs to remain balanced. You are going to work to keep your nervous system running smoothly, by acting on your senses so that the messages it receives, at least some of the time, are messages of calm, serenity and relaxation.

To relax your nervous system, try these ideas

- Prefer diffuse or dim lighting to bright lighting.
- Stay in the shade instead of spending long hours in the sun.
- Avoid ambient noise from sources like radio, TV, video games.
- Take a walk in the fresh air for at least 15 minutes a day, and do some deep breathing.
- Practice deep breathing exercises a number of times :

day.

- Avoid substance abuse (alcohol, stimulants, tobacco).
- Eat healthy food.
- Make full use of water (drink a lot, take showers every day, take a whirlpool or swim whenever possible).
- Relaxing means disconnecting yourself.
- Avoid all kinds of intense emotion: anger, resentment, jealousy, negative people, upsetting films or TV shows, stressful games.

Since you know yourself a little better by now, you also know what specific areas need special attention in your own life, depending on the kinds of habits you have developed over time. I should add one more point - never feel rushed. There's nothing more stressful than feeling rushed. You can't concentrate, you make mistakes, and what you have to do ends up taking twice as much time. So don't rush others, and never let others rush you.

In order to relax completely, you have to re-educate the muscles of your body. And when your muscles are completely relaxed, it becomes quite simply impossible to harbor any negative feelings or thoughts.

'I don't have time to relax'

How many people complain that they just don't have the time to relax, but waste precious minutes, adding up to hours each day, which could be used to mobilize their energies to fight the inevitable obstacles we all encounter? There are so many interesting and extremely enjoyable ways to relax, all sorts of hobbies, physical disciplines like yoga or t'ai chi, and so on. You could start a collection of music or books, or learn a new language.

Which activities will you find relaxing? Make a list of them here:

Above all, make an effort to master that most basic form of relaxation - breathing. This is the foundation of permanent relaxation. Train yourself to breathe properly.

The benefits of complete breathing

It's incredible, when you consider how important breathing is, to see so many people breathing badly, completely unconsciously, as if they didn't care a fig about staying healthy, allowing their lungs to shrivel and harden day by day. Fortunately there is a marvelous technique for overcoming the harmful effects of the air we breathe and keeping our blood rich in oxygen: complete abdominal breathing. You've already seen some of the benefits.

Try this exercise:

1. Breathe in gently, without moving your chest,

allowing the breath to lift your stomach. When your stomach is expanded to its maximum, and without stopping breathing in, continue inhaling and lift your rib cage. Then contract your stomach and lift the upper part of your chest, sending air to the upper limits of your lungs.

2. Now breathe out gently through your nose, pushing all the air out of your system.

Practicing this simple exercise will teach you breath control. You can gradually increase the time it takes to inhale and exhale, as well as holding your breath for short periods.

Summary

1. To live in a relaxed way you have to acquire a new outlook, a new sense of balance.

2. Although we need a certain amount of tension, we also need to relax.

3. Negative mental images are easy to find; we must make an effort to look for positive, relaxing ones.

4. There is only one way to get rid of tension: you must work on your nervous system and disconnect it.

5. Breathing is the key to relaxation, and is essential for relaxing your nervous system.

6. Relaxation allows you to benefit fully from the technique of suggestion.

Complete relaxation exercise

To relax your entire body start by finding a quiet place where you are not likely to be disturbed, if possible dimly lit. Remove your shoes, glasses, tie, and so on, and loosen any other restrictive clothing. Stretch out on your back with your arms by your sides. Don't cross your feet, clench your fists or tighten your jaw. There should be no noise around you.

Start by doing about a dozen breathing cycles:

- Step 1 Breathe in gently through your nose, lifting your stomach.
- Step 2 Without stopping, lift the middle part of your rib cage, keeping your stomach in its raised position.
- Step 3 Push the air up into the top of your lungs by continuing to inhale and expanding the upper part of your chest, this time pushing your stomach in and down.
- Step 4 Breathe out gently through your nose. When you reach the end of the exhalation make a little extra effort to get all the air out of your lungs. Then go back to Step I and repeat the cycle.

Next, close your eyes, and in a low voice talk to your entire body and relax it completely (or record your voice and play back the recording):

I am focusing my mind on my right arm ... my right

arm is gradually getting heavier ... heavier and heavier . .. my right arm is heavy ... my right arm is so heavy ... completely heavy, heavier and heavier.., it weighs so much, it is completely, totally heavy.

Now I'm focusing on the tips of my fingers.., and now on my left arm ... I'm concentrating on my left arm ... my left arm is gradually getting heavier.., heavier and heavier.., my left arm is heavy.., my left arm is so heavy.., my... left.., arm.., is ... so ... heavy ... completely ... heavy, heavier and heavier ... it is completely, totally heavy.

Now I focus my attention on the tips of my toes, and I can feel a vibration as cool air comes in contact with them. Now my right leg ... will soon grow heavier ... heavier and heavier ... my calf, my thigh is getting very heavy ... my right leg is getting heavier and heavier.., my... right...leg...is.., heavy... so heavy ... my right leg is completely and totally heavy.

Now I concentrate on my left leg ... I am relaxing my left leg ·.. and soon it will start getting heavier.., my left calf and thigh are getting heavier and heavier.., my left leg is so heavy ... my ... left...leg...is...so...heavy...heavy...completely, totally heavy.

My whole body feels heavy, heavier and heavier.., it weighs so much ... it is a heavy mass ... as if mercury were flowing through my veins instead of blood ... I abandon my body completely ... I can feel where my body touches the ground (or mattress, or carpet...) I can feel the point of contact.., and I am breathing freely, calmly and deeply.

Now I focus my attention on my right arm, and I feel a wave of heat flowing through it. My right arm is getting warm ... my right arm is getting hot ... it feels hot ... is hot ... hotter and hotter.., my right arm is so hot.., my...right...arm...is ... hot ... my right arm is burning hot ... completely hot.

Now I feel a gentle wave of heat flowing through my left arm ·.. my left arm is getting warmer.., my left arm is getting hotter and hotter.., it's so hot.., hot.., my left arm is burning hot... completely hot.

Now the wave of heat spreads down into my right leg.., warm blood circulates through my right leg ... my right leg is getting hotter.., hotter ... it's so hot ... hot ... my right leg is burning hot ... my right leg is burning hot ... it's completely hot.

Now I focus on my left leg.., it's getting hot.., my left leg is getting hotter and hotter.., so hot.., my left leg is very hot... my... left.., leg...is.., so... very.., hot.., so hot... completely hot.

Now the wave of heat. . heat. .flows through my body... my heart pumps hot blood through my whole body ·. my entire body is hot, hot ... I am relaxed ... I feel so relaxed ... more and more relaxed.., this feeling of relaxation spread through my entire body, growing larger and larger, closer and closer ... spreading into every muscle ... every cell of my body. I feel wonderfully relaxed ... and in this state of total relaxation I can rest.

(breathing)

When I open my eyes I will come out of this state of total relaxation and feel rested, refreshed, and completely reinvigorated ... my head, neck and shoulders will feel totally relaxed ... now I'm going to count to three, and on the count of three I will open my eyes:

One... two.., three.., and my eyes are open! I stretch like a cat, yawn, wriggle my toes and fingers, move my arms and legs, move my jaw up and clown as if I was chewing gum. I feel wonderful, rested, in harmony with myself, with others, with life and the entire universe. A new life is beginning for me!

WEEK 10 -- HAPPINESS

Well, here we are, the second to last chapter. You now know a lot more about the wealth of talents and abilities you possess. You've learned to make better use of some of them already, and in so doing have opened up new horizons which are far brighter and more attractive than those you were able to see before.

What you did a few weeks ago when you began this method was to take your first step through the doorway of happiness.

Now let's think a little more about what happiness means, and about perseverance, which is essential for attaining it.

You have probably noticed that a lot of people aren't happy. This is usually because they either don't want to be happy or don't know how to be happy.

Doing what is necessary to be happy

Does that sound a little too simple? Well, I can assure you that it's true. Although these people may not be consciously rejecting happiness, their behavior leads to the same end result: they don't do what is necessary to be happy. They may want to be happy, but they don't have the ability to discover for themselves what they have to do to be happy. They carry on blindly, guided by their instincts. Of course they know, theoretically at least, that pleasure and happiness are not one and the same thing. But they keep chasing after pleasure, setting themselves up for a fall time and time again.

So what is happiness?

Well, simply put, happiness is living in a state of harmony. Harmony with yourself, and with the people around you.

Creating harmony with yourself and with the entire universe

You get up one morning, open your window and find it's raining. You can't do anything about it. How are you going to react? If you start complaining about the lousy weather, muttering something like, 'Uurgh - don't tell me it's raining again!' you immediately become glum and morose, and set yourself up for a bad day. And this for no reason at all, because whatever you feel about it, whatever you say or don't say, will have absolutely no bearing on the weather.

If, on the other hand, you can get yourself into harmony with your environment - on this occasion a rainy day - then everything changes: although it may not be pleasant, the rain is at least acceptable. You get out your raincoat and umbrella, and make your way to work just as you do on a beautiful day.

When it rains, take a moment to observe the people you pass in the street. Some hurry along, all hunched over, their faces lined with tension, and you just know that they're wound up by it. Others walk along placidly, smiling despite the storm clouds. None of these people will get any more or any less wet because of the way they feel. But some will be unhappy, not because of the rain but because of the way they react to it, while others will be, if not completely ecstatic, at least comparatively less unhappy, which is in itself a way of being happy.

The same applies to heat in summer, cold in winter, the inconveniences of traveling, some unpleasant task you have to perform, power failures, the vicissitudes of professional life - in short, anything unpleasant that happens unexpectedly, in all of life's situations. And the best thing you can do for people you love is to simply be happy, and show them how you feel.

You must look inside yourself for the means to attain true happiness. The more you take control of your life, the better you are able to live in harmony with yourself and with others, to develop in harmony with your surroundings. And by so doing you place less emphasis on the false kinds of security that you may have based your happiness on in the past: material possessions, the prestige that comes with money or professional standing, and so on.

Acquire real security

You acquire real security as you manage to get rid of your negative feelings (hate, jealousy, worry, agitation, self pity). This, and only this, leads to true happiness.

What exactly are your goals? How about health, success and love of life? Not bad, I'd say. Well, the only thing negative feelings accomplish is to destroy the harmonious functioning of your body, and along with it your health. On the other hand, your positive feelings promote confidence and enthusiasm, attract the respect and esteem of others, and very often lead directly to great success and happiness.

For some people a positive frame of mind comes naturally. They have a positive temperament, and they received a positive education. And that is the best legacy any parent can leave their children. However, those people who are not naturally positive - in other words, whose subconscious is full of negativity - must and can acquire a positive outlook by making a conscious effort to do so.

Happiness can be learned

You can train yourself to be happy and optimistic just as you train your body through various physical exercises. Educators and parents can help train children to be joyous, content and happy, systematically get them used to seeing the bright side of things, to be curious about things, interested in all of nature's phenomena. In this way they are giving children the gift of joy and happiness, which will go a long way towards making them fulfilled as adults.

You create your own happiness or unhappiness yourself. There is no irrevocable destiny involved here, despite the fact that some people think there is. You can change your destiny by creating your own happiness. You and you alone are responsible. No one else can do it for you.

The miracle of being good-natured

One essential rule is that you must cultivate and maintain a good-natured attitude. This is one of the secrets of happiness. And just being good-natured can accomplish miracles: it can cure diseases, rid you of anxiety and instill you with a sense of confidence in yourself, in your abilities and undertakings, in life.

Each of us is really two people: one is negative, pessimistic, skeptical, easily tempted to fall into sloth, to denigrate other people, to be malevolent, jealous, angry. Fortunately we also have a positive side, a person who has faith in life, in truth, who is self-confident, enthusiastic, benevolent and tolerant of others. It is this positive side of yourself that you've been trying to develop over the last few weeks.

Eliminate negative feelings

Happiness can only be obtained by eliminating negative feelings: emotions generated by feelings of pessimism, timidity, anxiety, nervous tension, and so on, emotions which waste energy and paralyze action.

By developing your strong points, your positive points, you also eliminate your weak, negative points. So you have to become optimistic, enthusiastic, altruistic, confident, willful, persevering and courageous, and make yourself a more competent human being each day.

In this way you will accomplish everything you set out to do. You will develop and exploit the whole you, instead of using just a small part of your potential. You will learn to be yourself, making your life one harmonious unity.

Give your life meaning

Set yourself a single, lofty goal. It's not enough to want to get married and have children. Getting your children to do well in school is not a lofty ideal. Neither is supporting your family. These are all necessary steps along the way, but they are not ultimate goals.

What you need is a real goal. A goal that is so lofty, so difficult to attain that you'll have to spend your entire life trying.

An example of a worthy goal

One example of a goal worth pursuing is the constant and complete improvement of yourself. With a goal like that you won't find yourself with nothing left to do in the near future - you'll have enough work to occupy you for the rest of your days!

How will your epitaph read?

So you have to set a goal for yourself. You have to keep this goal firmly in mind at all times, and be able to say, 'I have a single goal in life.' This suggestion is the foundation upon which a life of greatness can be built. Without it, we often allow ourselves to get carried away by momentary distractions and worries, and to lose sight of what we really want.

If you are having trouble defining a single goal for yourself, why not think about what you'd like to see engraved on your tombstone and write it down here:

Are you doing all you can to be happy?

Would you like to know if you are taking the necessary steps to make yourself a happy person? If so, think about each of the following questions and answer as honestly as possible.

- Do I usually see the bright side of things?
- Do I accept events without complaining too much?
- How do I usually react to the inevitable?
- Do I make an effort to smile more? Be more benevolent?
- Am I satisfied with my life as it is?
- What is my goal in life? Is my goal a worthy enough one?
- Do I tend to start things and not finish them?
- Do I accept myself the way I am? Do I feel good about myself?
- Am I usually in a good mood, open-minded, ready to smile, sing, enjoy life?
- How much time do I devote each day to reading, conscious relaxation and suggestion?

- Do I have a lot of friends? Do people often ask me for advice?
- What am I planning to do in my old age?
- Are the people I live with happy?

To be happy you must be in harmony with yourself. You have to organize your life so that your acts, words and thoughts are in accordance with your major goal in life. It is when you are not in harmony that you fall prey to agitation, impatience, irritation, fear, regret, anxiety, and so on.

Now this does not mean you should suppress your true nature: to be in harmony with yourself you absolutely have to express your true nature, your true self, i.e. the subconscious collection of qualities you possess. To do this you have to train yourself, and the basis of this gradual training is the technique of conscious and voluntary autosuggestion.

It's not easy being an adult

It takes perseverance and tenacity, it's not easy being an adult. It's actually much easier to keep on living like a child, avoiding responsibilities, never taking control of your life. But if you want to be happy, you have to grow along with your body and become an adult human being.

This requires putting your lire in order: the way you think, work, play, in your personal hygiene, your sleeping habits, the way you organize your days, what you eat, and so on. It means changing yourself.

Without change progress is impossible.

If you don't make an effort to change yourself you'll just be like everyone else who doesn't care about their personal development. You can't even be physically healthy without change, without disciplining your life. You can't enjoy holidays and days off without disciplining your lire. You can't enjoy concerts, films, traveling or anything else as long as your personality is out of balance. You have nothing if you don't accept change. You have everything if your first concern in life is to simply be yourself.

If you don't like something change it!

Change is indispensable. You have to develop new positive habits to replace the old negative ones you've been living with for so long. In the past you may have been tense, nervous, agitated, negative, worrying about things for no reason, afraid of life. These are all habits. You've been working on changing them, and you've begun to live differently, not blaming yourself, trying to see the bright side of things, taking time to relax: these are also habits, and you must keep on making them stronger.

To be a happier person, develop your

being

It's never easy being a responsible adult. It takes perseverance and tenacity. You have to keep on striving and never give up. It takes faith and constancy to become a fulfilled human being. You must stick with it. You must continue striving to better yourself, at any cost, And to be certain that you will continue, you must adopt the necessary measures.

Happiness isn't something we possess, it's something we know, something we are. And developing your being can only make you a happier person. Knowing that although everything around you may crumble, your real self remains intact: that's what true happiness and real self-confidence is.

And as you acquire this assurance you begin to stand out from the masses of people who never ask questions, who never wonder about anything. You have already rid yourself of your false security, you are no longer satisfied with accepted truths and clichés. You could never be happy if you stopped now. There's no turning back.

Continue developing your mind

You have to keep on developing your mind. You've already learned a few things about the art of success by reading this book. Yet so many people don't bother reading!

It's incredible how reading has become a kind of luxury in modern times, reserved for those who have 'nothing better to do.'

Yet we make sure to eat well 3 times a day. We make an effort to eat well because we want to stay healthy. Well, the same goes for reading, you have to make an effort to nourish your mind, otherwise it too will die of hunger.

Summary

1. Happiness simply means living in a state of harmony.

2. Happiness is the certitude that even though, one day, I may be deprived of everything I own, I will lack nothing in myself.

3. Happiness resides in continued and integral self-improvement.

4. To be happy you need an ideal, a worthy goal which demands perseverance, the ability to change, and discipline. Because it isn't easy to be a fulfilled human being.

5. Happiness is feeling that you are getting somewhere, that you are growing, that you are accomplishing something.

WEEK 11 -- SUCCESS

To attain success you have to believe.

Today we're going to think about the climate necessary for happiness ... and for success.

We all want to be successful and happy in life. We also know that we can be happy and successful in life. But so many people simply do not have the basic and irreplaceable disposition that leads to success and happiness: believing in success, or in other words, being optimistic.

Believing in success is the required psychological component, the indispensable attitude for living out day-to-day lives.

Few people seem to realize that you have to believe in success in order to be happy. They seem to think that the ability to be happy is inherited - either you have it or you don't - and that you can't do anything to change things.

The hardest thing for people to learn is that they are the sum total of their thoughts, and that their environment, education and the kinds of thoughts they usually think have much more of an influence on their lives than their genes.

A belief in success can be cultivated! In order to live in a climate of faith and optimism, both of which are indispensable to happiness, we must fight two enemies: skepticism, and various emotional states which are hostile to being optimistic.

Let's take a closer look.

Skepticism is the beginning of faith

Suppose you begin an important task. You'll never be able to see it through if you doubt the possibilities of success right from the start.

If you are skeptical about the work on personal development that you are about to undertake, how can you hope to carry it through to a successful conclusion? If you don't believe in yourself, how can you expect others to believe in you?

If you are skeptical all the time, you are not living in a climate conducive to happiness. It's a little like walking around with a ball and chain attached to your leg.

Use your reason to acquire or maintain faith in

yourself. Think about the real possibility of your success. Transmit this message to the depths of your being through the technique of suggestion. Remind yourself that you do have what it takes to succeed, that there is a hidden potential inside you, just waiting for an opportunity to break out into the light of day.

You create your own destiny

No one can prevent you from developing yourself. You create your own destiny.

Repeat frequently: 'Everything is easy for those who can see their future dream as a present reality.'

It is useless and even harmful to dwell on mistakes you made in the past, or about the disappointments you have to deal with in your day-to-day lire. You mustn't draw these things out. It's much better to simply tally up what you learned, remember what is useful and forget about the rest ... and get busy moving on to something else.

States which are hostile to optimism

First of all there are the various depressive states - sadness, apathy, anxiety or boredom. Look for the cause. Once you've found it you can remedy the situation by taking a shower or doing a session of complete relaxation.

If you can't find the cause, there is really only one

thing to do: spend some energy. Take a walk in the fresh air, play the piano, sing, fix something around the house, write, talk to a friend. In other words, get busy doing something else. Train yourself not to let your occasional feelings of sadness, anxiety, aimlessness or worry affect you too much. And if you feel really sad, go ahead and have a good cry, and then move on. Crying can do you a lot of good.

Then there are impulsive states, the most common being anger and nervousness (irritation, overwork). The only tactic to combat these can be summed up in one word: wait. Step in and create a gap between the emotion and action; take the time necessary to re-examine the situation and regain control, for example the time it takes to do twenty deep breathing cycles.

As for anger, sarcasm, impatience, irritation, you must act on your exterior body in order to calm your inner state (remember that the physical and mental sides of human beings are deeply united). One thing you can do is remain silent for as long as it takes to recover your inner calm and equilibrium.

Never act under the influence of emotion

There's an old saying that goes, 'Count to ten when you're angry, count to a hundred when you're very angry.'

Never act under the influence of a strong emotion. Instead, reach for one of the life-jackets we suggested, don't move around too much, and hold on, just like a sailor weathering a storm.

Also be careful about what you say. Don't make any long speeches or useless confessions. Avoid wasting your energy on complaining about your problems and worries. Work on keeping your exterior calm: walk slowly, don't slam any doors, don't raise your voice. Of course, despite all these precautions, you will still get angry or impatient, but you will succumb to the emotion much less often. These simple and natural techniques, deep breathing, exterior calm and so on, can and will work wonders, adding immeasurably to your inner peace. It's quite extraordinary, and yet so simple.

Opening up to others

Being open means living in a climate of optimism and faith in yourself, which in turn leads you to cultivate habits conducive to happiness.

And because you have faith in yourself, others will believe in you too. And these 'others' are extremely important in the pursuit and maintenance of your happiness. We cannot live our lives completely on our own, we need the support of other people. Thus it becomes very important to get ourselves into harmony with all those who can help us build our happiness.

Happiness can only exist for those who have faith in the possibility of being happy and who are open to others.

Imagine how much happiness you can achieve, now that you've spent all these weeks moving ahead on the road to success!

Of course, you won't be miraculously transformed by this method, but it will place you in a position to make your life a wonderful adventure, and to attain success.

What is success? Success is a 'succession' of goals which you set for yourself, and which you attain. So to attain success all you have to do is:

1. set goals (specific goals with a reasonable time limit);
2. believe in success;
3. attain your goals, or learn from your failures;
4. set new goals.

The impossible has almost become possible!

Let's stop for a moment, since we have arrived at the final chapter, and take a short look back at what we've covered so far.

Because, in fact, it's very important to take an occasional time out and ask yourself: where was I headed? Where am I headed now? What progress have I made? What obstacles did I encounter? How can I avoid these problems in future? How am I doing as far as my personal development is concerned? These are all questions we should consider carefully.

Thinking ... how important it is to reflect, to think about things. Because we don't think enough, out mistakes don't help us as they should. And because we don't evaluate out actions, we don't make progress. Taking a step back is not a waste of time, but rather a springboard towards higher achievements.

The ten principles of success

The things we come up with while taking stock of ourselves should be written down. There's no better way to organize your mind than to write down your thoughts. It makes self-expression easier, and helps us to be objective about ourselves. I recommend regular sessions devoted to writing down your thoughts: whenever you feel embarrassed or bored, when you're looking for the cause of a problem or of a negative emotion, and so on. In this final chapter we'll take a brief look at the principle of living we have discovered together over the last few weeks, and which have helped us take control of our lives.

1. I either adapt or I die. In order to adapt I fraternize with people and I act.

2. I am worth a hundred times more than I think.

3. Changing my exterior personality changes my inner being.

4. I react, and then act.

5. Enthusiasm can change the world. It is the spark of greatness that resides in all of us.

6. I will always be myself.

7. I will start being the person I want to be right now.

8. I can't control my thoughts if I don't control my body.

9. I create my own happiness and unhappiness.

10. I believe in who I am and in what I do.

Can you add anything more to the list?

Taking stock of yourself

Would you like to know how far you've come, now that you've reached the end of this book? Answer the following questions as honestly as you can:

[]Yes [] No

Am I able to relax better than before?

[]Yes [] No

Has my health improved?

[]Yes [] No

Am I better equipped to make my own decisions?

[]Yes [] No

Do I find it easier to carry things through?

[]Yes [] No

Do I have more of an influence on the people around me?

[]Yes [] No

Have my friends noticed a change in me?

[]Yes [] No

Do I tend to live up to my commitments more than in the past?

[]Yes [] No

Am I thinking more?

[]Yes [] No

Have I mentioned the method to people I think might benefit from it?

[]Yes [] No

Do I tend to see the positive side of events more now than in the past?

[]Yes [] No

Am I more enthusiastic?

[]Yes [] No

Am I more interested in the human condition?.

[]Yes [] No

Am I able to confide in people more easily?

[]Yes [] No

Do I have more friends?

[]Yes [] No

Am I able to adapt more easily than before?

[]Yes [] No

Do I feel better about myself?

[]Yes [] No

Do I feel more comfortable expressing myself in front of other people?

[]Yes [] No

Would I like to continue my training in this area?

[]Yes [] No

Total out of 20

[ ]Yes [ ] No

Summary

1. We are the sum total of our thoughts.

2. I must believe in myself.

3. To do this I must avoid skepticism and other states of mind which are hostile to optimism, such as depression, impulsiveness, and so on.

4. If I have faith in myself, others will have faith in me.

5. No person is an island.

CONCLUSION

You've come a long way in these eleven weeks. But you can't rest on your laurels! Keep at it, persevere until you succeed, and then strive to make yourself even better.

The list of suggested reading that follows will help you progress even further. And remember, others have trodden the same path before you.

Your potential is infinite. And now you have the practical means to keep developing and exploiting it. As I am wont to say to many of my students, 'There is a single word written on the door to success: open!'

SUGGESTED READING

Fisher, Mark (1998), The Instant Millionaire, Sigdgwick and Jackson.

Fisher, Mark, and Mark Allen (1998), How to Think Like a Millionaire, New World Library.

Godefroy, Christian H. (1993), Super Health: How to Control Your Body's Natural Defences, Piatkus Books.

Godefroy, Christian H. (1998), Mind Power.

Godefroy, Christian H. (1997), How to Cope with Difficult People.

Hill, Napoleon (1975), Think and Grow Rich, Fawcett Books.

Maltz, Maxwell (1994), Psycho-Cybernetics, Bantam Books.

Robbins, Anthony (1992), Awaken the Giant Within,

Pocket Books.

MORE

If you'd like to find more texts on self-help and ways to improve the way you live through self-growth, you can find a wealth of info on the positive club web site. Membership is free, and you'll find free books of self-help.

http://positive-club.com

CPSIA information can be obtained
at www.ICGtesting.com
Printed in the USA
LVHW052247060721
692003LV00012B/1690